THE CAREER IDEAS FOR KIDS SERIES

Second Edition

DIANE LINDSEY REEVES
with
LINDSEY CLASEN

Illustrations by
NANCY BOND

Ferguson
An imprint of Infobase Publishing

CAREER IDEAS FOR KIDS WHO LIKE ADVENTURE AND TRAVEL, Second Edition

Ferguson
An imprint of Infobase Publishing
132 West 31st Street
New York NY 10001

Library of Congress Cataloging-in-Publication Data

Reeves, Diane Lindsey, 1959–
  Career ideas for kids who like adventure and travel / Diane Lindsey Reeves; with Lindsey Clasen; illustrations by Nancy Bond. — 2nd ed.
    p. cm — (Career ideas for kids series)
  Includes bibliographical references and index.
  ISBN-13: 978-0-8160-6547-9 (hardcover)
  ISBN-10: 0-8160-6547-0 (hardcover) 1. Vocational guidance—Juvenile literature. 2. Adventure and adventurers—Vocational guidance—Juvenile literature. [1. Adventure and adventurers——Vocational guidance. 2. Vocational guidance.] I. Clasen, Lindsey. II. Title.
  HF5381.2.R428 2007
  331.702—dc22   2007002713

Original text and cover design by Smart Graphics
Illustrations by Nancy Bond

Printed in the United States of America

MP Hermitage 10 9 8 7 6 5 4 3 2 1

This book is printed on acid-free paper.

CONTENTS

A million thanks to those who took the time to invest in young lives by sharing their stories about work and providing their photos for this book:

Michele Abrate
Douglas Allen
Todd Arnold
Martha Culp
Susan Dziama
Mike Gersh
Tom Goodpaster
Kirby Green
Michael Harney
Chuck Hunter
Joan E. Higginbotham
Tracee Kelly
Shelley Matheny
Aaron Marcus
Alison Smale

Finally, much appreciation and admiration is due to all the behind-the-scenes people at Ferguson who have done so much to make this series all that it is. With extra thanks to James Chambers and Sarah Fogarty.

MAKE A CHOICE!

Choices.

You make them every day. What do I want for breakfast? Which shirt can I pull out of the dirty-clothes hamper to wear to school today? Should I finish my homework or play video games?

Some choices don't make much difference in the overall scheme of things. Face it; who really cares whether you wear the blue shirt or the red one?

Other choices are a major big deal. Figuring out what you want to be when you grow up is one of those all-important choices.

But, you say, you're just a kid. How are you supposed to know what you want to do with your life?

You're right: 10, 11, 12, and even 13 are a bit young to know exactly what and where and how you're going to do whatever it is you're going to do as an adult. But it's the perfect time to start making some important discoveries about who you are, what you like to do, and what you do best. It's a great time to start exploring the options and experimenting with different ideas. In fact, there's never a better time to mess around with different career ideas without messing up your life.

When it comes to picking a career, you've basically got two choices.

CHOICE A

You can be like lots of other people and just go with the flow. Float through school doing only what you absolutely have to in order to graduate, take any job you can find, collect a paycheck, and meander your way to retirement without making much of a splash in life.

Although many people take this route and do just fine, others end up settling for second best. They miss out on a meaningful education, satisfying work, and the rewards of a focused and well-planned career. That's why this path is not an especially good idea for someone who actually wants to have a life.

CHOICE B

Other people get a little more involved in choosing a career. They figure out what they want to accomplish in their lives— whether it's making a difference, making lots of money, or simply enjoying what they do. Then they find out what it takes to reach that goal, and they set about doing it with gusto. It's kind of like these people do things on purpose instead of letting life happen by accident.

Choosing A is like going to an ice cream parlor where there are all kinds of awesome flavors and ordering a single scoop of plain vanilla. Going with Choice B is more like visiting that same ice cream parlor and ordering a super duper brownie sundae drizzled with hot fudge, smothered in whipped cream, and topped with a big red cherry.

Do you see the difference?

Reading this book is a great idea for kids who want to go after life in a big way. It provides a first step toward learning about careers that match your skills, values, and dreams. It will help you make the most out of your time in school and maybe even inspire you to—as the U.S. Army so proudly says—"be all that you can be."

Ready for the challenge of Choice B? If so, read the next section for instructions on how to get started.

HOW TO USE THIS BOOK

This book isn't just about interesting careers that other people have. It's also a book about interesting careers that you can have.

Of course, it won't do you a bit of good to just read this book. To get the whole shebang, you're going to have to jump in with both feet, roll up your sleeves, put on your thinking cap—whatever it takes—to help you do these three things:

☼ Discover what you do best and enjoy the most. (This is the secret ingredient for finding work that's perfect for you.)

☆ Explore ways to match your interests and abilities with career ideas.

☆ Experiment with lots of different ideas until you find the ideal career. (It's like trying on all kinds of hats to see which ones fit!)

Use this book as a road map to some exciting career destinations. Here's what to expect in the chapters that follow.

GET IN GEAR!

First stop: discover. These activities will help you uncover important clues about the special traits and abilities that make you *you*. When you are finished you will have developed a personal Skill Set that will help guide you to career ideas in the next chapter.

TAKE A TRIP!

Next stop: explore. Cruise down the career idea highway and find out about a variety of career ideas that are especially appropriate for people who like travel and adventure. Use the Skill Set chart at the beginning of each career profile to match your own interests with those required for success on the job.

Once you've identified a career that interests you, kick your exploration into high gear by checking out some of the Web sites, library resources, and professional organizations listed at the end of each career profile. For an extra challenge, follow the instructions for the Try It Out activities.

MAKE A DETOUR THAT TAKES YOU PLACES!

Here's your chance to explore up-and-coming opportunities that could take you around the globe and give you ideas to help you blaze an exciting new career trail.

DON'T STOP NOW!

Third stop: experiment. The library, the telephone, a computer, and a mentor—four keys to a successful career planning adventure. Use them well, and before long you'll be on the trail of some hot career ideas of your own.

WHAT'S NEXT?

Make a plan! Chart your course (or at least the next stop) with these career planning road maps. Whether you're moving full steam ahead with a great idea or get slowed down at a yellow light of indecision, these road maps will keep you moving forward toward a great future.

Use a pencil—you're bound to make a detour or two along the way. But, hey, you've got to start somewhere.

HOORAY! YOU DID IT!

Some final rules of the road before sending you off to new adventures.

SOME FUTURE DESTINATIONS

This section lists a few career planning tools you'll want to know about.

You've got a lot of ground to cover in this phase of your career planning journey. Start your engines and get ready for an exciting adventure!

GET IN GEAR!

Career planning is a lifelong journey. There's usually more than one way to get where you're going, and there are often some interesting detours along the way. But you have to start somewhere. So rev up and find out all you can about one-of-a-kind, specially designed you. That's the first stop on what can be the most exciting trip of your life!

To get started, complete the five exercises described throughout the following pages.

DISCOVER #1: WATCH FOR SIGNS ALONG THE WAY

Road signs help drivers figure out how to get where they want to go. They provide clues about direction, road conditions, and safety. Your career road signs will provide clues about who you are, what you like, and what you do best. These clues can help you decide where to look for the career ideas that are best for you.

Complete the following statements to make them true for you. There are no right or wrong answers. Jot down the response that describes you best. Your answers will provide important clues about career paths you should explore.

Please Note: If this book does not belong to you, write your responses on a separate sheet of paper.

On my last report card, I got the best grade in_____ .

On my last report card, I got the worst grade in_____ .

I am happiest when _____ .

Something I can do for hours without getting bored is _____ .

Something that bores me out of my mind is_____ .

My favorite class is _____ .

My least favorite class is _____ .

The one thing I'd like to accomplish with my life is _____ .

My favorite thing to do after school is

_____ .

My least favorite thing to do after school is _____ .

Something I'm really good at is_____ .

Something really tough for me to do is _____ .

My favorite adult person is _____ because _____ .

When I grow up _____.

The kinds of books I like to read are about _____.

The kinds of videos I like to watch are about _____ .

DISCOVER #2: RULES OF THE ROAD

Pretty much any job you can think of involves six common ingredients. Whether the work requires saving the world or selling bananas, all work revolves around a central **purpose** or reason for existing. All work is conducted somewhere, in some **place**, whether it's on the 28th floor of a city skyscraper or on a cruise ship in the middle of an ocean. All work requires a certain **time** commitment and is performed using various types of **tools**. **People** also play an important part in most jobs—whether the job involves interacting with lots or very few of them. And, especially from where you are sitting as a kid still in school, all work involves some type of **preparation** to learn how to do the job.

Another word for these six common ingredients is "values." Each one represents important aspects of work that people value in different ways. The following activity will give you a chance to think about what matters most to you in each of these areas. That way you'll get a better idea of things to look for as you explore different careers.

Here's how the process works:

First, read the statements listed for each value on the following pages. Decide which, if any, represent your idea of an ideal job.

Next, take a look at the grid on page 16. For every value statement with which you agreed, draw its symbol in the appropriate space on your grid. (If this book doesn't belong to you, use a blank sheet of paper to draw your own grid with six big spaces.) Or, if you want to get really fancy, cut pictures out of magazines and glue them into the appropriate space. If you do not see a symbol that represents your best answer, make up a new one and sketch it in the appropriate box.

When you are finished, you'll have a very useful picture of the kinds of values that matter most to you in your future job.

❤	❏	I want to help other people.	

PURPOSE

Which of the following statements describes what you most hope to accomplish in your future work? Pick as many as are true for you and feel free to add others.

❤	❏	I want to help other people.
💵	❏	I want to make lots of money.
★	❏	I want to do something I really believe in.
✋	❏	I want to make things.
🧠	❏	I want to use my brain power in challenging ways.
💡	❏	I want to work with my own creative ideas.
🏆	❏	I want to be very successful.
🪜	❏	I want to find a good company and stick with it for the rest of my life.
🔦	❏	I want to be famous.

Other purpose-related things that are especially important to me are

PLACE

When you think about your future work, what kind of place would you most like to do it in? Pick as many as are true for you and feel free to add others.

	❑	I want to work in a big city skyscraper.
	❑	I want to work in a shopping mall or retail store.
	❑	I want to work in the great outdoors.
	❑	I want to travel a lot for my work.
	❑	I want to work out of my own home.
	❑	I want to work for a government agency.
	❑	I want to work in a school or university.
	❑	I want to work in a factory or laboratory.

Other place-related things that are especially important to me are

TIME

When you think about your future work, what kind of schedule sounds most appealing to you? Pick as many as are true for you and feel free to add others.

	❑	I'd rather work regular business hours—nine to five, Monday through Friday.
	❑	I'd like to have lots of vacation time.
	❑	I'd prefer a flexible schedule so I can balance my work, family, and personal needs.
	❑	I'd like to work nights only so my days are free.
	❑	I'd like to work where the pace is fast and I stay busy all day.
	❑	I'd like to work where I would always know exactly what I'm supposed to do.
	❑	I'd like to work where I could plan my own day.
	❑	I'd like to work where there's lots of variety and no two days are alike.

Other time-related things that are especially important to me are

TOOLS What kinds of things would you most like to work with? Pick as many as are true for you and feel free to add others.			
	☐	I'd prefer to work mostly with people.
	☐	I'd prefer to work mostly with technology.
	☐	I'd prefer to work mostly with machines.
	☐	I'd prefer to work mostly with products people buy.
	☐	I'd prefer to work mostly with planes, trains, automobiles, or other things that go.
	☐	I'd prefer to work mostly with ideas.
	☐	I'd prefer to work mostly with information.
	☐	I'd prefer to work mostly with nature.

Other tool-related things that are especially important to me are

PEOPLE

What role do other people play in your future work? How many do you want to interact with on a daily basis? What age group would you most enjoy working with? Pick as many as are true for you and feel free to add others.

	❏	I'd like to work with lots of people all day long.
	❏	I'd prefer to work alone most of the time.
	❏	I'd like to work as part of a team.
	❏	I'd like to work with people I might choose as friends.
	❏	I'd like to work with babies, children, or teenagers.
	❏	I'd like to work mostly with elderly people.
	❏	I'd like to work mostly with people who are in trouble.
	❏	I'd like to work mostly with people who are ill.

Other people-related things that are especially important to me are

 	❏	I want to find a job that requires a college degree.
	❏	I want to find a job where I could learn what I need to know on the job.
	❏	I want to find a job that requires no additional training after I graduate from high school.
	❏	I want to find a job where the more education I get, the better my chances for a better job.
BOSS	❏	I want to run my own business and be my own boss.

PREPARATION

When you think about your future work, how much time and energy do you want to devote to preparing for it? Pick as many as are true for you and feel free to add others.

Other preparation-related things that are especially important to me are

Now that you've uncovered some word clues about the types of values that are most important to you, use the grid on the following page (or use a separate sheet of paper if this book does not belong to you) to "paint a picture" of your ideal future career. Use the icons as ideas for how to visualize each statement. Or, if you'd like to get really creative, get a large sheet of paper, some markers, magazines, and glue or tape and create a collage.

PURPOSE	PLACE	TIME

TOOLS	PEOPLE	PREPARATION

DISCOVER #3: DANGEROUS DETOURS

Half of figuring out what you do want to do is figuring out what you don't want to do. Get a jump start on this process by making a list of 10 careers you already know you absolutely don't want to do.

Warning: Failure to heed early warnings signs to avoid careers like this can result in long hours of boredom and frustration spent doing a job you just weren't meant to do.

(If this book does not belong to you, make your list on a separate sheet of paper.)

1. _____   _____

2. _____   _____

3. _____   _____

4. _____   _____

5. _____   _____

6. _____   _____

7. _____   _____

8. _____   _____

9. _____   _____

10. _____   _____

Red Flag Summary:
Look over your list, and in second column above (or on a separate sheet of paper) see if you can summarize what it is about these jobs that makes you want to avoid them like a bad case of cooties.

DISCOVER #4: ULTIMATE CAREER DESTINATION

Imagine that your dream job is like a favorite tourist destination and you have to convince other people to pick it over every other career in the world. How would you describe it? What features make it especially appealing to you? What does a person have to do to have a career like it?

Take a blank sheet of paper and fold it into thirds. Fill each column on both sides with words and pictures that create a vivid image of what you'd most like your future career to be.

Special note: Just for now, instead of actually naming a specific career, describe what your ideal career would be like. In places where the name of the career would be used, leave a blank space like this _____. For instance: For people who want to become rich and famous, being a _____ is the way to go.

DISCOVER #5: GET SOME DIRECTION

It's easy to get lost when you don't have a good idea of where you want to go. This is especially true when you start thinking about what to do with the rest of your life. Unless you focus on where you want to go, you might get lost or even miss the exit. This discover exercise will help you connect your own interests and abilities with a whole world of career opportunities.

Mark the activities that you enjoy doing or would enjoy doing if you had the chance. Be picky. Don't mark ideas that you wish you would do. Mark only those that you would really do. For instance, if skydiving sounds appealing but you'd never do it because you are terrified of heights, don't mark it.

Please Note: If this book does not belong to you, write your responses on a separate sheet of paper.

❏ 1. Rescue a cat stuck in a tree
❏ 2. Visit the pet store every time you go to the mall
❏ 3. Paint a mural on the cafeteria wall
❏ 4. Send e-mail to a "pen pal" in another state
❏ 5. Survey your classmates to find out what they do after school
❏ 6. Run for student council
❏ 7. Try out for the school play
❏ 8. Dissect a frog and identify the different organs
❏ 9. Play baseball, soccer, football, or _____ (fill in your favorite sport)

❏ 10. Talk on the phone to just about anyone who will talk back

❏ 11. Try foods from all over the world—Thailand, Poland, Japan, etc.

❏ 12. Write poems about things that are happening in your life

❏ 13. Create a really scary haunted house to take your friends through on Halloween

❏ 14. Recycle all your family's trash

❏ 15. Bake a cake and decorate it for your best friend's birthday

❏ 16. Simulate an imaginary flight through space on your computer screen

❏ 17. Build model airplanes, boats, doll houses, or anything from kits

❏ 18. Sell enough advertisements for the school yearbook to win a trip to Walt Disney World

❏ 19. Teach your friends a new dance routine

❏ 20. Watch the stars come out at night and see how many constellations you can find

❏ 21. Watch baseball, soccer, football, or _____ (fill in your favorite sport) on TV

❏ 22. Give a speech in front of the entire school

❏ 23. Plan the class field trip to Washington, D.C.

❏ 24. Read everything in sight, including the back of the cereal box

❏ 25. Figure out "who dunnit" in a mystery story

❏ 26. Take in stray or hurt animals

❏ 27. Make a poster announcing the school football game

❏ 28. Put together a multimedia show for a school assembly using music and lots of pictures and graphics

❏ 29. Think up a new way to make the lunch line move faster and explain it to the cafeteria staff

❏ 30. Invest your allowance in the stock market and keep track of how it does

❏ 31. Go to the ballet or opera every time you get the chance

❏ 32. Do experiments with a chemistry set

❏ 33. Keep score at your sister's Little League game

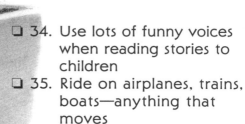

34. Use lots of funny voices when reading stories to children
35. Ride on airplanes, trains, boats—anything that moves
36. Interview the new exchange student for an article in the school newspaper
37. Build your own treehouse
38. Help clean up a waste site in your neighborhood
39. Visit an art museum and pick out your favorite painting
40. Make a chart on the computer to show how much soda students buy from the school vending machines each week
41. Keep track of how much your team earns to buy new uniforms
42. Play Monopoly in an all-night championship challenge
43. Play an instrument in the school band or orchestra
44. Take things apart and put them back together again
45. Write stories about sports for the school newspaper
46. Listen to other people talk about their problems

❏ 47. Imagine yourself in exotic places
❏ 48. Hang around bookstores and libraries
❏ 49. Play harmless practical jokes on April Fools' Day
❏ 50. Join the 4-H club at your school
❏ 51. Take photographs at the school talent show
❏ 52. Create an imaginary city using a computer
❏ 53. Do 3-D puzzles
❏ 54. Make money by setting up your own business—
paper route, lemonade stand, etc.
❏ 55. Keep track of the top 10 songs of the week
❏ 56. Read about famous inventors and their inventions
❏ 57. Make play-by-play announcements at the school
football game
❏ 58. Answer the phones during a telethon to raise
money for orphans
❏ 59. Be an exchange student in another country
❏ 60. Write down all your secret thoughts and favorite
sayings in a journal
❏ 61. Jump out of an airplane (with a parachute, of course)
❏ 62. Plant and grow a garden in your backyard (or
windowsill)

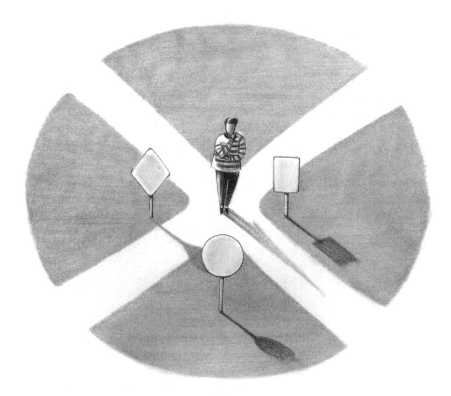

❏ 63. Use a video camera to make your own movies
❏ 64. Spend your summer at a computer camp learning lots of new computer programs
❏ 65. Build bridges, skyscrapers, and other structures out of LEGOs
❏ 66. Get your friends together to help clean up your town after a hurricane or other natural disaster
❏ 67. Plan a concert in the park for little kids
❏ 68. Collect different kinds of rocks
❏ 69. Help plan a sports tournament
❏ 70. Be DJ for the school dance
❏ 71. Learn how to fly a plane or sail a boat
❏ 72. Write funny captions for pictures in the school yearbook
❏ 73. Scuba dive to search for buried treasure
❏ 74. Recognize and name several different breeds of cats, dogs, and other animals
❏ 75. Sketch pictures of your friends

❏ 76. Answer your classmates' questions about how to use the computer
❏ 77. Draw a map showing how to get to your house from school
❏ 78. Pick out neat stuff to sell at the school store
❏ 79. Make up new words to your favorite songs
❏ 80. Take a hike and name the different kinds of trees, birds, or flowers
❏ 81. Referee intramural basketball games
❏ 82. Join the school debate team
❏ 83. Make a poster with postcards from all the places you went on your summer vacation
❏ 84. Write down stories that your grandparents tell you about when they were young

CALCULATE THE CLUES

Now is your chance to add it all up. Each of the 12 boxes on the following pages contains an interest area that is common to both your world and the world of work. Follow these directions to discover your personal Skill Set:

1. Find all of the numbers that you checked on pages 18–23 in the following boxes and mark

them with an X. Work your way all the way through number 84.

2. Go back and count the Xs marked for each interest area. Write that number in the space that says "Total."

3. Find the interest area with the highest total and put a number one in the "Rank" blank of that box. Repeat this process for the next two highest scoring areas. Rank the second highest as number two and the third highest as number three.

4. If you have more than three strong areas, choose the three that are most important and interesting to you.

Remember: If this book does not belong to you, write your responses on a separate sheet of paper.

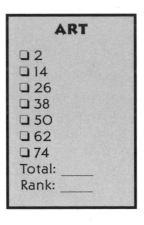

ADVENTURE

❑ 1
❑ 13
❑ 25
❑ 37
❑ 49
❑ 61
❑ 73
Total: _____
Rank: _____

ART

❑ 2
❑ 14
❑ 26
❑ 38
❑ 50
❑ 62
❑ 74
Total: _____
Rank: _____

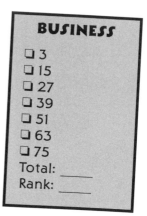

BUSINESS

❑ 3
❑ 15
❑ 27
❑ 39
❑ 51
❑ 63
❑ 75
Total: _____
Rank: _____

COMPUTERS

- ❏ 4
- ❏ 16
- ❏ 28
- ❏ 40
- ❏ 52
- ❏ 64
- ❏ 76

Total: _____
Rank: _____

HISTORY

- ❏ 5
- ❏ 17
- ❏ 29
- ❏ 41
- ❏ 53
- ❏ 65
- ❏ 77

Total: _____
Rank: _____

MATH

- ❏ 6
- ❏ 18
- ❏ 30
- ❏ 42
- ❏ 54
- ❏ 66
- ❏ 78

Total: _____
Rank: _____

MUSIC/DANCE

- ❏ 7
- ❏ 19
- ❏ 31
- ❏ 43
- ❏ 55
- ❏ 67
- ❏ 79

Total: _____
Rank: _____

SCIENCE

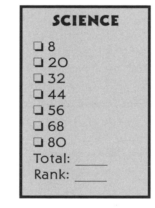

- ❏ 8
- ❏ 20
- ❏ 32
- ❏ 44
- ❏ 56
- ❏ 68
- ❏ 80

Total: _____
Rank: _____

SPORTS

- ❏ 9
- ❏ 21
- ❏ 33
- ❏ 45
- ❏ 57
- ❏ 69
- ❏ 81

Total: _____
Rank: _____

TALKING

- ❏ 10
- ❏ 22
- ❏ 34
- ❏ 46
- ❏ 58
- ❏ 70
- ❏ 82

Total: _____
Rank: _____

TRAVEL

- ❏ 11
- ❏ 23
- ❏ 35
- ❏ 47
- ❏ 59
- ❏ 71
- ❏ 83

Total: _____
Rank: _____

WRITING

- ❏ 12
- ❏ 24
- ❏ 36
- ❏ 48
- ❏ 60
- ❏ 72
- ❏ 84

Total: _____
Rank: _____

What are your top three interest areas? List them here (or on a separate piece of paper).

1. _____

2. _____

3. _____

This is your personal Skill Set and provides important clues about the kinds of work you're most likely to enjoy. Remember it and look for career ideas with a Skill Set that matches yours most closely. You'll find a Skill Set box at the beginning of each career profile in the following section.

TAKE A TRIP!

Cruise down the
career idea highway
and enjoy in-depth
profiles of some of the interesting options in this field. Keep
in mind all that you've discovered about yourself so far. Find
the careers that match your own Skill Set first. After that,
keep on trucking through the other ideas—exploration is
the name of this game.

This book covers career ideas from two directions: those
for people with the travel bug and those for the adventur-
some at heart. On the travel side, there are many opportunities for basing an entire career on travel, transportation,
or some aspect of the tourism and hospitality business.
On the adventure side, challenge, daring, and going far
beyond the call of duty are common ingredients in some
of these careers. Many require much more physical stamina than a "regular" job. Quite often the warmth and security of an office is replaced by work in the great outdoors.
Adventure-packed careers can be good choices for people
who shudder at the thought of a nine-to-five job. They can

also provide meaningful ways to make a difference and help others. Many are high on challenge and low on boredom.

Do you want a career with on-the-job training? Want to see the world while you work? Take a look at some of the careers that follow and get ready for the adventure of your life!

Also, as you read about the following careers, imagine yourself doing each job and ask yourself the following questions:

☀ Would I like it?
☀ Would I be good at it?
☀ Is it the stuff my career dreams are made of?

If so, make a quick exit to explore what it involves, try it out, check it out, and get acquainted! Look out for the symbols below.

Buckle up and enjoy the trip!

 TRY IT OUT

 CHECK IT OUT

 ON THE WEB

 AT THE LIBRARY

 WITH THE EXPERTS

A NOTE ON WEB SITES

Internet sites tend to move around and change a bit. If you have trouble finding a particular site, use an Internet browser to find a specific Web site or type of information.

Airport Personnel

WHAT ARE AIRPORT PERSONNEL?

Airport personnel include anybody and everybody who works at an airport. Starting with the parking attendants and baggage handlers who greet passengers as they arrive at the airport and ending with the pilots and flight attendants who get passengers where they need to go, there are many people who work to keep air travel safe and comfortable.

Pilots have the high-profile job of flying all kinds of sophisticated aircraft loaded with people and cargo. It takes a lot of skill and training to earn the trust of the thousands of people who board planes each day. The pilot's job begins an hour before the actual flight; two hours before if it is an international flight. This time is used to go over the flight plan, check weather conditions, brief the rest of the crew, and thoroughly check the airplane to make sure that everything is working properly. A commercial flight will usually have two pilots: a captain and a copilot who work in a cockpit filled with powerful computer systems and high-tech equipment. The captain is in charge and supervises the rest of the crew. The captain and the copilot share the job of flying the plane. They work as a team especially during

takeoff and landing, which are the most complicated parts of any flight.

Commercial airline pilots are required by the Federal Aviation Administration (FAA) to have an airline transport pilot's license. To qualify, a pilot has to be at least 23 years old and have at least 1,500 hours of flying experience. They also have to pass a written FAA test as well as flight examinations. Major airlines like pilots to have some college; some even require a degree in an aviation-related field.

Some pilots enroll in a flight school or a university that has an aviation program. Over time, they build up the hours and different ratings necessary to fly for the major airlines. Others get the training and experience they need with the military.

Flight attendants are responsible for the safety and comfort of a flight's passengers. Like the pilots, their jobs begin about an hour before each flight. They are briefed about the flight by the captain and make sure that all the emergency equipment is in good working order and that the passenger cabin is in tip-top shape. They greet the passengers and help them find their seats. Before the plane takes off, the flight attendants go over all the safety features of the plane and let the passengers know what they need to do in case of an emergency.

During the flight, the attendants serve the passengers a snack or meal. However, the job requires much more than serving food and drinks. One of the most important parts of a flight attendant's job is never seen by most passengers. This responsibility involves doing whatever it takes to keep things on track during bad weather, medical emergencies, or other types of sky-high calamities. This aspect of the job took on even more importance in the aftermath of the September 11 terrorist attacks. Flight attendants go through even more safety training so that they are ready to respond to anything that might happen in flight.

Flight attendants are a cheerful bunch and have to be experts at dealing with people, even difficult ones. Passengers have more contact with flight attendants than with any other airline employees, so attendants need to be customer service experts.

Flight attendants don't need a college degree, but it doesn't hurt. They should be very personable, poised, and professional. Some airlines have height and weight requirements. Flight attendants who are fluent in one or more foreign languages have a leg up on choice international flights. Airlines put new flight attendants through an intense training program that lasts several weeks.

Aircraft mechanics are the important folks who keep those big birds running safely. They fix things that aren't working properly and perform scheduled preventative maintenance in accordance with FAA guidelines. Aircraft mechanics work under a lot of pressure. A lot of lives depend on their getting the job done correctly and quickly. Most aircraft mechanics are trained at one of about 200 trade schools that are licensed by the FAA.

Although **reservation agents** don't see much of the passengers, they often provide passengers with that all-important first impression of the airline. That's because reservation agents are the people who provide flight information such as schedules, fares, and availability. By phone, they make flight reservations, assign seats, and take payments. Reservation agents usually have high school degrees. They need both computer and people skills. Specialized training can be obtained through any number of reputable travel schools or the airlines themselves.

Ticket agents manage the airline counters. They check in passengers, process baggage, confirm or make seat assignments, and sell tickets. To qualify for this type of job, people need a high school degree, the ability to communicate well, and strong computer skills. Since they're the ones who deal with the fallout when a plane is delayed or rerouted, a healthy dose of patience is often useful when dealing with irritated, and sometimes irate, customers.

Pilots and flight attendants have the most high-profile jobs, and they obviously do the most traveling. Other airline employees don't travel as part of their jobs, but they do receive flight benefits that allow them to fly for free or at dramatically reduced prices.

Airport employees should be prepared to live near a major airline hub such as Dallas, New York, Atlanta, Los Angeles, or Chicago. Since airlines run 24 hours a day, seven days a week, all airport employees can expect to work some crazy hours—especially during the holidays or other peak flying times.

It's hard to get a feel for an entire industry in one short chapter, especially one that involves so many interesting career options. If you're really interested in working for an airline someday, take off and do some research on your own.

☞ TRY IT OUT

HOW PLANES FLY

The very idea that airplanes can get up and stay up in the air is mind-boggling. Find out more about how it happens at these Web sites:

- Beginners Guide to Aerodynamics at http://www.gre.nasa.gov/WWW/K-12/airplane/bga.html
- How Stuff Works at http://travel.howstuffworks.com/airplane.htm
- Science Fun with Airplanes at http://www.ag.ohio-state.edu/~flight

Use what you discover to create a poster illustrating how planes fly.

ADVANCE RESERVATIONS

Get some practice being a reservation agent with some of these online travel Web sites:

- ☼ Cheap Tickets at http://www.cheaptickets.com
- ☼ Orbitz at http://www.orbitz.com
- ☼ Travelocity at http:/www.travelocity.com

Use these online reservation systems to check out fares between different locations and airlines. Enter different places, times, and dates. Make note of how the day, the time, and the amount of advance notice you give affects the fare. Also, check and see how much extra it costs to fly first class. Try to find the best deal and make a chart showing your results.

 CHECK IT OUT

🖱 ON THE WEB

UP, UP AND AWAY

Take a virtual airplane or helicopter for a spin at some of these Web sites:

- ☼ *Bump Copter2* at http://www.learn4good.com/ games/simulation/bump_copter_2.htm
- ☼ *Final Approach* at http://mypage.direct.ca/b/ bsimpson/finalapp.html

Also, make a pit stop at http://www.avkids.com where you'll find all kinds of games and activities.

Make sure to keep a flight log to keep track of your online airborne experiences!

ONLINE TRAVEL

While you're online, check out some of these interesting airline sites.

- ☼ Find out more about the fathers of flight, Wilbur and
  Orville Wright, at http://www.first-to-fly.com.
- ☼ Visit the Federal Aviation Administration (FAA) Kid's
  Web site at http://www.faa.gov/education_research/
  education/educator_resources/educators_corner/
  index.cfm?item-kid.
- ☼ See what's happening at your favorite airport right
  now via live online video at http://www.ags.uci
  .edu/~tmheaney/SNA/cameras.htm or http://www
  .fly.faa.gov/flyfaa/usmap.jsp.

 ## AT THE LIBRARY

BOOK A FLIGHT

Delve into the different careers in the airline industry by
checking out some of these books:

Careers in Focus: Travel and Hospitality. New York: Ferguson,
2006.
Discovering Careers for Your Future: Transportation. New
York: Ferguson, 2001.
Minden, Cecilia. *Pilots.* Chanhassen, Minn.: Child's World,
2006.
Payment, Simone. *Cool Careers Without College for People
Who Love to Travel.* New York: Rosen, 2003.
Tetrick, Byron. *Choosing a Career as a Pilot.* New York: Rosen,
2001.

WITH THE EXPERTS

Airline Dispatchers Federation
2020 Pennsylvania Avenue NW, #821
Washington, DC 20006-1811
http://www.dispatcher.org

Airline Pilots Association
1625 Massachusetts Avenue NW
Washington, DC 20036-2204
http://www.alpa.org

Air Transport Association of America
1301 Pennsylvania Avenue NW, Suite 1100
Washington, DC 20004-1707
http://www.airlines.org

Association of Flight Attendants-CWA
501 Third Street NW
Washington, DC 20001-2760
http://www.afanet.org

Professional Aviation Maintenance Association
400 Commonwealth Drive
Warrendale, PA 15096-7511
http://www.pama.org

GET ACQUAINTED

Mike Gersh,
Airport Personnel

CAREER PATH

CHILDHOOD ASPIRATION: To
be a pilot.

FIRST JOB: Working construction on an indoor soccer arena.

CURRENT JOB: Air traffic controller at the Atlanta Center, the
world's busiest air traffic control
facility.

HIGH-FLYING AMBITION

From the time Mike Gersh was in kindergarten he loved
planes. He says that one of his aunts still has his early draw-

ings of airplanes and helicopters. As a military "brat" who moved with his family to different army posts every two or three years, he had plenty of opportunities to see planes in action, especially when his dad was stationed at a pilot training post.

At age 18, realizing that his grades were not quite high enough to get into a good college, he joined the Air Force. His dad's experience as a military recruiter came in handy as Gersh negotiated his way to a guaranteed slot in air traffic control. Gersh seized this opportunity as a means to reach his ultimate goal of becoming a fighter pilot. He knew that he'd have to work extra hard, earn a college degree, and become a commissioned officer in order to meet the air force's strict requirements for pilots. After earning a degree in management, he was well on his way to realizing this dream when an injury made it necessary to come up with a new plan.

PLAN B

Fortunately for Gersh, his military air traffic experience paved the way for opportunities in the civilian world. While other new air traffic controllers must go through a five-year process of tests and training administered by the Federal Aviation Administration (FAA), Gersh was ready to hit the ground running. He landed a position at the Atlanta Center and has made a fascinating career out of guiding airplanes into and out of the sky.

He doesn't work in a control tower at Atlanta's Hartfield-Jackson International Airport like one might expect. Air traffic controllers who work in towers are responsible for planes flying in a five-mile radius around the airport. Once airplanes are six miles out, they are "handed off" to approach control, another group of air traffic controllers, who guide the planes 40 miles out.

At that point, Gersh and his colleagues at the Atlanta Center take over and handle all aircraft flying in a huge region that includes parts of Georgia, South Carolina, North Carolina, Tennessee, Kentucky, Mississippi, and Alabama. Instead of working in a tower where they can actually see

planes coming, Gersh and his colleagues work in a dark radar room where hundreds of planes are represented by blips on a computer screen.

Think of the sky as a "giant pie," suggests Gersh, and it will help explain how the air traffic system works. Each type of air traffic control station owns a little piece of the sky. Gersh's slice involves lining up planes en route to the Atlanta airport in a way that assures their safe arrival. He first makes contact with pilots when they are a couple hundred miles away.

TOO CLOSE FOR COMFORT

No two days are alike in Gersh's work, but his goal as an air traffic controller is always the same: to keep a five-mile circle or "bubble skirter" around each plane. Five miles is the magic number designated by the FAA as the distance planes need to safely stay out of each other's way. With 3.25 million planes flying in and out of the Atlanta airport every year, you'd think that the task would be nearly impossible. But Gersh says that out of all those flights they only had 95 close calls last year, and none of those were in danger of crashing. When planes get too close, it's Gersh's job to give them more wiggle room. He does this by directing pilots to slow down, make a slight turn, climb higher, or fly lower.

AROUND THE CLOCK

Perhaps one of the most unpredictable things about Gersh's work is his schedule. Since airplanes fly 24/7, air traffic controllers have to be there to guide them in. Since he gets Tuesdays and Wednesdays off, Gersh says that his Monday is actually a Thursday. Some days he works from 4:00 P.M. until midnight, other days from midnight to 6:00 A.M., and other days from noon to 8:00 P.M. It takes some getting used to but Gersh says he likes the variety.

In his spare time, he likes to fly around in his own private plane. It's not a fighter jet, of course, but it still gives Gersh a chance to enjoy the wide, blue yonder.

Astronaut

WHAT IS AN ASTRONAUT?

10, 9, 8 . . . Are you looking for career that's out of this world? 7, 6, 5, 4 . . . Have you ever wondered what it's like up there with the stars? 3, 2, 1 . . . Do you wonder what it would be like to be an astronaut and blast off into space? Astronauts (from the Greek words for "star sailor") are the men and women who explore the vast frontiers of outer space. They work to discover more about other planets, the sun and moon, and other galaxies. They investigate how and if life can exist in these different environments. Just like yesterday's cowboys explored the Wild West, today's astronauts explore the unknown reaches of the universe.

One of the most fascinating space projects now in the works involves creating an international space station that would allow astronauts from around the world to actually live on another planet. Astronauts living at this station will conduct experiments, explore other planets, and attempt to uncover many of the mysteries of outer space. Can you imagine someday sending a postcard from Mars to your friends on Earth? It could happen in your lifetime!

Currently, all U.S. astronauts work for the National Aeronautics and Space Administration (NASA). The biggest project now underway is the Space Transportation System, also known as the space shuttle, which flies missions into orbits around Earth. Each mission includes a commander, or pilot, who is responsible for flying the spacecraft; payload specialists, who are responsible for conducting the scientific investigations and specialized activities contracted for by sponsors of the mission; and various mission specialists. Astronauts from other countries sometimes join the group, but a shuttle team is limited to eight people.

When shuttle astronauts go into space, they are launched into an orbit 115 to 250 miles above Earth, where they travel more than 17,000 miles per hour and circle the globe every 90 minutes. That means they see the Sun rise or set every 45 minutes. By all accounts, it is a completely amazing experience!

Although astronauts play the most visible role in these missions, they would never leave Earth without the support of vast numbers of people on the ground. This support team includes aerospace engineers (who design, test, and build the systems and spacecraft), microgravity specialists, and mission control center experts. After the shuttle lands, other specialists and engineers inspect the shuttle for damage from its reentry into Earth's

atmosphere and get it ready for the next flight. Teamwork is the key to making it all happen.

It isn't easy to become an astronaut. Although more than 4,000 people apply for these coveted positions, only 100 people are chosen every two years to go to NASA headquarters for interviews and extensive medical and psychological testing. Only 20 candidates make the final cut and actually go into astronaut training.

To qualify, you must meet vision and height minimums and have at least a bachelor's degree in engineering, science, or math plus three years of relevant experience. Most of those selected have advanced degrees in their field of expertise. Pilots usually are chosen from the ranks of the U.S. Air Force or another military branch. Good grades are a must, as is being in tip-top physical shape. Speaking more than one language is a plus. Not just anyone can withstand the pressures of being cooped up in a tiny spaceship thousands of miles from home, so NASA looks long and hard to find applicants who have the right stuff.

If you hope to get your shot at becoming an astronaut, you might as well start now by reading everything you can get your hands on about space, astronauts, rocket science, and NASA. Keep your grades up and stay in shape. Also, investigate some of the other occupations related to the space industry and see if you find other options for your talents and ambitions—just in case.

If you are one of the lucky ones who make the cut, you can expect to spend years training for what is likely to be just a few days or weeks in space. The first round of rigorous training lasts for a year and tends to weed out the wannabes from the real astronauts. Those who make it through that initial hurdle train constantly to learn new things about how equipment and systems work as well as how their bodies will function in space. They spend time experiencing zero gravity or working in a huge swimming pool practicing with their equipment while dressed in their bulky space suits. Before it's over, their training will have covered scuba diving, parachuting, land and sea survival training, shuttle systems, science, and technology. Tons of time is spent simulating all kinds of situations that could occur while they are in space. Every possibility and every stage of the launch are considered and practiced over and over again.

It's not easy, but it can certainly be exciting. Considering that space travel is a relatively new accomplishment, there is still much work to be done to discover the many wonders of the universe. Who knows what kinds of opportunities your generation will have to continue this incredible quest on behalf of humankind?

TRY IT OUT

COUCH POTATO ASTRONAUTS
Rent movies like *The Right Stuff*, *Apollo 13*, and *From the Earth to the Moon*. Pretend that you are an astronaut and have to report to mission control about what you learned from watching one or more of these movies. Write up your observations and be ready to give an out-of-this-world presentation.

SPACE VACATIONS
Can't wait to become an astronaut? Then you'd better start saving your pennies for a week at Space Camp. Space Camp has locations in Alabama, California, and Florida, and offers a variety of awesome astronaut training programs for kids from the ages of 9 through 18. The program generally involves simulated space shuttle missions, training simulators (like the 1/6 gravity chair), rocket building and launching, and all kinds of scientific experiments. For all the details, go online to http://www.spacecamp.com.

SOLAR SYSTEM
Before you venture off into the wild blue yonder, get acquainted with the terrain. Find out all you can about the solar system and follow the instructions found at http://www.exploratorium.edu/ronh/solar_system to make a model of the solar system.

For inspiration while you work, listen to real astronauts tell their stories at http://www.pbs.org/wgbh/nova/tothemoon.

✔ CHECK IT OUT

🖱 ON THE WEB
A CYBERSPACE MISSION
Find all kinds of online space adventures at some of these Web sites sponsored by the National Aeronautics and Space Administration (NASA):

- ☿ Astro-Venture at http://quest.arc.nasa.gov/projects/astrobiology/astroventure/avhome.html
- ☿ NASA Education Home Page at http://www.nasa.gov/audience/forkids/home/index.html
- ☿ NASA for Kids at http://www.nasa.gov/audience/forkids/kidsclub/flash/index.html.
- ☿ NASA Quest at http://quest.arc.nasa.gov
- ☿ Return to Flight at http://ksnn.larc.nasa.gov/intro.htm
- ☿ Space Place at http://spaceplace.jpl.nasa.gov/en/kids
- ☿ SpaceKids at http://spacekids.hq.nasa.gov/osskids
- ☿ StarChild at http://starchild.gsfc.nasa.gov/docs/StarChild/StarChild.html

📚 AT THE LIBRARY
WALK A MILE IN THEIR SPACESHOES

Briggs, Carole S. *Woman Space Pioneers*. Minneapolis: Lerner, 2005.

Goldberg, Jan. *James Lovell: The Rescue of Apollo 13*. New York: Rosen, 2004.

Gueldenpfenning, Sonia. *Spectacular Women in Space*. Toronto, Ont.: Second Story Press, 2005.

Iverson, Ellen. *Ellen Ochoa: Hispanic-American Biographies*. New York: Raintree, 2005.

Mattern, Joanne. *Sally Ride: Astronaut*. New York: Ferguson, 2005.

Orr, Tamra. *Alan Shepard: First American in Space*. New York: Rosen, 2004.

Raum, Elizabeth. *Buzz Aldrin: American Lives*. Portsmouth, N.H.: Heinemann, 2005.

———. *John Glenn: American Lives.* Portsmouth, N.H.: Heinemann, 2005.

———. *Neil Armstrong: American Lives.* Portsmouth, N.H.: Heinemann, 2006.

Saari, Peggy. *Space Exploration Biographies.* Farmington Hills, Mich.: UXL, 2004.

WITH THE EXPERTS

National Aviation Hall of Fame
PO Box 31096
Dayton, OH 45437-0096
http://www.nationalaviation.org

National Aeronautical Association
1737 King Street, Suite 220
Alexandria, VA 22314-2760
http://www.naa.aero

National Aeronautics and Space Administration
NASA Headquarters, Suite 5K39
Washington, DC 20546-0001
http://www.nasa.gov

GET ACQUAINTED

Joan E. Higginbotham, Astronaut

CAREER PATH

CHILDHOOD ASPIRATION:
To be an engineer.

FIRST JOB: Babysitting.

CURRENT JOB: NASA astronaut.

LOVE AT FIRST SIGHT

Joan Higginbotham went to college planning to be an electrical engineer. She'd even picked out the company she wanted to work for when she graduated—IBM—but it wasn't hiring when she was ready to start work. Then along came some recruiters from NASA. They made it sound like an interesting place to work, so Higginbotham took a trip to actually see the launch pad and the shuttle for herself. "It was like something out of *Star Wars*. I felt a keen sense of excitement just seeing it. That was when I decided I absolutely had to be an astronaut."

Her first assignment was to work on the team that launches the shuttle. While she was working, she earned master's degrees in management and space systems. Considering Higginbotham's experience and education, her friends thought she'd make a good astronaut and encouraged her to apply for the training program. She followed their advice, went through the interview process, and made it!

"This is an incredibly great place to work," Higginbotham says. "Women are given the same opportunities as the men, the same training, the same pay. It's a lot of hard work, and we're kept constantly busy." The only thing she sometimes regrets is not having more time to just relax.

NEVER A DULL MOMENT

Training is a big part of Higginbotham's job. One of her favorite training exercises involves experiencing the feeling of zero gravity. The exercise involves climbing steeply to high altitudes in a KC135 aircraft. At a certain point during the climb, there is a 20- to 25-second window of time in which she feels weightless. As the plane levels out and then descends sharply at the same angle as the climb, she floats. "It's an incredible feeling, and I love it," she says.

Astronaut training involves all kinds of challenging experiences. One day Higginbotham may find herself immersed in a huge tank of water dressed in her spacesuit, and putting together complex equipment. Another day she might be sitting in a simulator, blasting off into "virtual" space.

Higginbotham explains that during these flight simulations, "they throw in every kind of failure they can think of to train us so we can anticipate, plan, and react effectively and efficiently."

Other training involves water survival, parachute jumping, scuba diving, and learning to fly a T-38 jet plane. "This was the hardest part for me—learning to fly at Mach One in the jet. It was such a new experience." Of course, working out every day (including weight and cardiovascular training) to keep in top physical condition is part of the job as well.

In addition to all this training, she works on learning Russian so she can function effectively with her international colleagues in the space station. She has also traveled to Russia (Moscow and Star City) to train with Russian cosmonauts, and was fascinated to observe both the similarities and the differences of life in another country.

OUT-OF-THIS-WORLD ADVICE

Higginbotham says that aspiring astronauts have to get great grades in school. Math and science skills are key in this profession, but so is getting a well-rounded education by taking all kinds of courses. Astronauts work as a team, so you have to work well with others—knowing when to lead and when to follow. You also need the self-confidence to get through any challenge and to be able to think fast in a constantly changing, dynamic environment.

If you want to be an astronaut, Higginbotham urges you to learn all you can about space as you finish school. She says it takes a lot of drive to get to work on the space shuttle. You have to really, really want it, and you have to work hard to get there. And getting there is just the beginning.

Commercial Fisher

SKILL SET

✔ ANIMALS & NATURE

✔ TRAVEL

✔ ADVENTURE

SHORTCUTS

GO fishing!

READ *Eyewitness: Fish* by Steve Parker and Dave King (New York: DK Eyewitness Books, 2005).

TRY going online to http://www.nmfs.noaa.gov/pr/education/kids/htm where you'll find all kids of "fishy" information.

WHAT IS A COMMERCIAL FISHER?

Gone fishing! It's the rallying cry of weekend fishers everywhere. But grabbing a fishing pole and some worms isn't what commercial fishing is about. Commercial fishers bring in tons of fish each year—sometimes braving rough seas and harsh weather to satisfy the world's seafood lovers.

It takes several things to be a commercial fisher: First, of course, fishers need access to lots of water and plenty of fish. That's why many fishers tend to live near oceans. But finding fish isn't always easy. Fishers have to know a lot about the habits of fish—where they travel and when. And fishers also have to follow specific government regulations as they try to make a living.

Weather is another contributing factor to a fisher's livelihood. Although there's not a thing anyone can do about it, weather often makes the difference between a successful year of fishing and a complete washout. Even in the best of circumstances, commercial fishers encounter bouts of nasty weather that make the job all the more challenging. Weather also guides fishing patterns and locations. For instance, herring spawn might be the "catch of the day" during the winter months, while halibut are plentiful in the spring. Some fishers work only during the summer or winter months. Others work year-round, although that sometimes means going to where the fish are at different times of the year—maybe it's Alaska in the summer and Seattle during the winter.

Commercial Fisher

Water, fish, and weather cover the basic "tools" of the trade, but there are two other important factors: one is the boat and the other is people to buy the fish. The first is sometimes harder to come by than the second. That's because boats are very expensive to buy and maintain, which is why most commercial fishers don't own their own boats but instead work for companies or other people who do.

As for people to buy the fish, that's a whole industry in and of itself. Fishers generally make an arrangement with one or more seafood processing plants that bring their catch to market. In some places in the world, fish is a daily part of people's diets. In America, some types of fish are considered a delicacy, while others, like tuna and salmon, are more common.

In the United States, Alaska is the fishing "hot spot." According to the National Marine Fisheries Service, there were 9,756 registered fishing vessels and thousands of people working in Alaska's commercial fishing industry in 2006 (although not all of these people actually catch fish).

As for training, more often than not commercial fishing is a trade that's learned on the job. Like farming and other types of strenuous, outdoor occupations, fishing is one of those careers that some people thrive on. In some fishing towns, it is not uncommon for fishing to go back several generations in certain families. Women as well as men are found on commercial fishing vessels everywhere. Fishing is certainly an equal opportunity employer. Any good fisher needs the stamina to work long hours, a respect for the wily ways of nature, and a willingness to work hard.

Those people interested in the more scientific and technical aspects of the fishing industry might choose to pursue a college degree in fisheries science or commercial fish harvesting. Another option is to learn about vessel operations through a program that specializes in maritime studies, or to get safety training by joining the U.S. Coast Guard.

☞ TRY IT OUT

GO FISH!

You may not have access to a commercial fishing vessel or even one of those charter fishing boats that are so popular in many tourist areas, but you can start your fishing career with just a rod and a good-sized pond or lake. Ask a parent or trusted adult to take you fishing, and see what you think. If it's your first time out for a good catch, go online for some fishing tips at http://familyfun.go.com and search for "a beginner's guide to fishing."

No fishing expedition is complete without cleaning the fish and enjoying a fresh fish dinner!

FISHING FOR EMPLOYMENT

To get a look at all the different jobs available in the fishing industry, visit these two Web sites:

☸ Seafood Industry Jobs Network at http://www
.fishjobs.com
☸ Alaska Fishing Jobs at http://www.alaskafishingjobs.com

Take note of the skills required for each type of job, the salary, the locations of various jobs, and compare what you think are the best opportunities.

KA-CHING!

Follow the money and find out the going rate for fish today. Go online to Fishery Market News at http://www.st.nmfs.gov/st1/market_news/index.html and compare how much Boston fishers are getting for lobster with what Gulf fishers are getting for shrimp. This Web site includes up-to-date prices of everything from clams to whiting. If a pound of lobster goes for $3.40, how much would you get for a ton? Set up your own virtual fish market and make a price list of what it will cost per pound for at least five varieties of fish.

 # CHECK IT OUT

ON THE WEB

FISHING FOR FUN

While the educational value of some of the following Web sites may be questionable, they'll provide a few minutes of fun as you learn more about sea life and fishing.

- Fish'n Kids Resources at http://www.fishnkids.com
- The Fish Olympics at http://www.liverpoolmuseums.org.uk/nof/fish
- Marine Life Learning Center at http://www.fishid.com/facts.htm
- U.S. Fish and Wildlife Service Especially for Kids at http://www.fws.gov/kids

 ## AT THE LIBRARY

FISHING FOR BOOKS

Champion, Neil. *Seas and Oceans: Caring for the Planet.* North Mankato, Minn.: Smart Apple Media, 2006.

Day, Trevor. *Lakes and Rivers: Biomes of the Earth.* New York: Facts On File, 2006.

———. *Oceans: Biomes of the Earth.* New York: Facts On File, 2006.

Helbrough, Emma. *Ocean Life.* Farmington Hills, Mich.: Black-birch, 2006.

Littlefield, Cindy. *Sea Life Games and Puzzles.* North Adams, Mass.: Storey, 2007.

Llewellyn, Claire. *Survive at Sea: Survivor Challenge.* New York: Silver Dolphin, 2006.

Morrison, Marianne. *Mysteries of the Sea: How Divers Explore the Ocean Depths.* Washington, D.C.: National Geographic, 2006.

Wilkes, Sarah. *Fish.* Milwaukee, Wisc: Gareth Stevens, 2006.

🗣 WITH THE EXPERTS

American Fisheries Society
5410 Grosvenor Lane
Bethesda, MD 20814-2199
http://www.fisheries.org/afs

American Fishermen's Research Foundation
PO Box 992723
Redding, CA 96099-2723
http://www.afrf.org

Deep Sea Fishermen's Union
5215 Ballard Avenue NW
Seattle, WA 98107-4838
http://www.dsfu.org

Fishermen's Marketing Association
320 Second Street, Suite 2B
Eureka, CA 95501-0457
http://www.trawl.org

National Fisheries Institute
7918 Jones Branch Drive, Suite 700
McLean, VA 22102-3319
http://www.aboutseafood.com

Women's Fisheries Network
2442 NW Market Street, #243
Seattle, WA 98107-4137
http://www.fis.com/wfn

GET ACQUAINTED

Kirby Green,
Commercial Fisher

CAREER PATH

CHILDHOOD ASPIRATION:
To be a fisherman.

FIRST JOB: Working on his dad's boat one summer in exchange for a BMX bike.

CURRENT JOB: Commercial fisherman.

LIKE FATHER, LIKE SON

Kirby Green was born on a small fishing island in Alaska, where his father was a fisherman. He and his family lived there, miserable winters and all, until his mother put her foot down and insisted that they move somewhere with a more comfortable climate. Hawaii seemed to fit the bill, so the family moved there when Green was eight. His father spent the summers fishing in Alaska and would often let Green tag along.

Green loved fishing, but once he graduated from high school he thought he should give something else a try, just to be sure fishing was what he really wanted to do with his life. He decided that teaching might be a good thing for him to consider. He spent two years in college and then returned to his first love—the ocean.

It took some scrimping and saving and lots of hard work, but by the time Green was 21 years old he'd managed to get enough cash together to put a down payment on his own boat. The Janet G is his pride and joy. Built in 1929 and 56 feet long, the boat holds 50,000 pounds of fish.

FISHER'S HOURS

Green and his crew fish in Alaskan waters from June through September. On a good day, the crew can fill Janet G in a couple of hours; other times it takes a couple of days. Either way, these months are filled with long hours and hard work.

This schedule gives Green several months off to knock around and do other things from his home base in Seattle. Travel consumes as much free time as Green's schedule and budget will allow. Otherwise, the time is filled working on the Janet G, working out at the gym, and doing repairs for other businesses around town. He has also managed to earn a college degree from the University of Washington and is working toward a master's degree. He plans to teach elementary school in the winters and fish in the summers.

A BAD FISH DAY

It's a bad day when you go out on your boat and don't catch enough fish to pay the costs of fuel and broken equipment. And it's a bad day when the weather gets crazy and you have to struggle to stay afloat. Some days are like that, but most of them aren't.

As with most jobs, fishing has both good and bad points. On Green's list, the pros far outweigh the cons. Of course, the job gets dangerous at times, and you can get tired of working with the same four or five people all day. However, working outdoors and enjoying some of the most amazing scenery in the world is a cool way to make a living. Green says it's pretty exciting on those days when you set your nets once and end up with 30,000 to 40,000 pounds of fish. It can also be fun just to goof off on board the ship or just to relax and let your mind wander. Those things you can't very well do in a typical office environment.

Green admits that fishing is one of those careers that you either love or hate. Lucky for Green, fishing is it for him!

Cruise Director

SHORTCUTS

GO to a travel agency and get some cruise line brochures. Check out the different kinds of activities each offers.

READ *Ship* by Brian Lavery (New York: DK Publishing, 2004).

TRY taking a course in public speaking.

SKILL SET

✔ TRAVEL
✔ TALKING
✔ ADVENTURE

WHAT IS A CRUISE DIRECTOR?

Cruising on a luxurious ship to exotic places all over the world is a dream vacation for all kinds of people—newlyweds enjoying their honeymoons, families creating memories, older folks making the most of their retirement years, and young singles looking for fun. No matter why they set sail, taking a cruise is expensive, and people come aboard expecting to get their money's worth. It's the cruise director's job to make sure that all passengers enjoy their experiences.

Think of a cruise ship as a luxurious resort that floats. These ships have all the amenities of the grandest hotel and more. A cruise ship has wonderful accommodations, incredible food, and nonstop activities—and that's just the beginning. Add lots of pools and outdoor sports, at least one theater, a health club, and several nightclubs, and you've got the makings of quite a vacation. Daily entertainment might include a Broadway-type stage show, line dancing with a DJ, a formal gala, a comedy show, a magic show, karaoke, and several different styles of bands.

Still looking for something to do? How about some fun and games such as bingo, scavenger hunts, talent shows, and trivia contests? Then, of course, there are exciting days to be spent in port with plenty of shopping and sightseeing for all.

So what does a cruise director have to do with all this? Everything! A cruise director is responsible for all the planning,

scheduling, and hiring it takes to keep things hoppin' on board a cruise ship. Fortunately, cruise directors don't have to do all the work themselves. Instead, they manage a fairly large staff of assistants and entertainers.

A cruise director's job starts long before the first passenger boards the ship. All of the activities have to be dreamed up, thoroughly planned, staffed, and scheduled. Entertainment options must offer something for everyone, from swinging singles to senior citizens and everyone in between. This means planning some "generic" activities that appeal to all as well as some specific to the different groups represented on the ship.

Once the planning is done and the ship sets sail, the real work begins! A daily schedule of events is distributed to passengers every day. With a variety of activities running nearly 24 hours a day, it's not hard to imagine the many hours a cruise director works while at sea.

Cruise directors often set the tone for an entire cruise. Their high-profile duties run the gamut from calling bingo games and warming up audiences for special performances to hosting cocktail parties. A winning personality and great people

skills are at the top of the list of required job skills. Cruise directors must be cool, calm, and collected as they respond to situations that would send most people into a tailspin. Grumpy customers? Smile and deal with it. Four days of bad weather with no end in sight? Smile and make the most of it. A major act in the entertainment lineup cancels at the last minute? Smile and make sure the show goes on without a hitch.

It's a big job and one that's not for everyone. But the job does come with some very attractive perks. Traveling to all kinds of exciting places tops the list. Then there's the fact that cruise directors tend to be paid pretty well. They also have their own cabins on the ship and eat the same great food that the passengers pay big bucks to enjoy.

A college degree is not required to become a cruise director, but a degree in public relations or hospitality certainly looks good on a resume and often gives a needed edge over other applicants. Proficiency in a foreign language is also helpful as is lots of public speaking experience.

Of course, no one gets a job as a cruise director without putting in some time in other areas of the ship. It's called paying your dues, and it's all part of getting the experience needed to handle all the responsibilities assigned to a cruise director. Many cruise directors start out as entertainers or youth counselors on board and work their way up to assistant cruise director. Landing the plum job as cruise director can take several years.

☞ TRY IT OUT

VIRTUAL CRUISE DIRECTOR

When it comes to cruising, kids have it made with a wide variety of programs tailored especially for their sea-going pleasure. Make a chart comparing the programs available for kids of various ages at the following cruise lines:

☼ Camp Carnival, with programs for kids from ages two to 17, at http://www.carnival.com/CMS/Onboard_ Activities/Generic-Camp_Carnival.aspx

- Disney Cruises, with activities for little kids, big kids, and teens, at http://disneycruise.disney.go.com/dcl/en_US/index?bhcp=1 (click on "you")
- Royal Caribbean Adventure Ocean at http://www.royalcaribbean.com (click on "activities" then click on "young adventurers") for links to programs for kids of all ages
- Princess Cruises Fun Zone at http://www.princess.com/onboard/activities/youthandteens for a boatload of activities for toddlers through teens

Make sure to list the best features offered by each company. When you are finished, put together all of their best ideas and some of your own to come up with a description of the ultimate cruise experience for kids your age.

A FAMILY AFFAIR

Plan some activities for your next family get-together. Think of some games that everyone will enjoy. Charades, anyone? Also, plan some specific activities for children, teenagers, moms and dads, and the older folks. Get some planning tips online at http://www.family-reunion.com. Use poster board and magic markers to create and decorate a schedule for a fun-filled day for the entire family. Be sure to include creative ideas for recording special memories of the event for future generations to enjoy.

✔ CHECK IT OUT

🖱 ON THE WEB

AHOY, MATEY!

Get your sea legs by learning more about a variety of these seaworthy subjects:

- Boat Safe Kids at http://www.boatsafe.com/kids/navigation.htm
- Kids and Boating at http://www.diybob.com/kidsa.htm

- ☼ International Maritime Signal Flags at http://www .44mlb.com/inter-maritime-signal-flags.htm and http://www.sartori.com/nhc/flags/
- ☼ National Maritime Center Kids Corner at http:// www.nauticus.org/gamespuzzles.html
- ☼ Sailing Through Science at http://www.goals.com/ ClassRm/SailSci/SailSciF.htm
- ☼ Sea Education Adventures at http://www.sdmaritime .com/contentpage.asp?ContentID=100
- ☼ Semaphore Flags at http://www.44mlb.com/kids semaphore.htm and http://www.sartori.com/ nhc/flags
- ☼ U.S. Maritime Administration Just for Kids at http:// www.marad.dot.gov/education/Kids

SEA TALK
People who spend time at sea have a language all their own. Get acquainted with navigation and maritime terms at Web sites such as:

- ☼ http://www.fortogden.com/nauticalterms.html
- ☼ http://www.lavasurfer.com/info/cruiseterms
- ☼ http://www.trans-inst.org/seawords.htm

AT THE LIBRARY

THE INSIDE SCOOP
Set sail for the library and check out some of these books on ships, navigation, and famous sea-going adventures (and misadventures):

Amato, William. *Cruise Ships.* New York: Powerkids, 2002.
Cook, Peter and David Salariya. *You Wouldn't Want to Sail on the Mayflower!* Danbury, Conn.: Franklin Watts, 2005.
Dickinson, Rachel. *Tools of Navigation: A Kid's Guide to the History and Science of Finding Your Way.* Anchorage, Alaska: Nomad, 2005.
Kentley, Eric. *Eyewitness: Boat.* New York: DK Eyewitness Books, 2000.

MacDonald, Fiona. *You Wouldn't Want to Sail with Christopher Columbus*. Danbury, Conn.: Franklin Watts, 2004.

Smith, A.G. *Where Am I: The Story of Maps and Navigation*. New York: Stoddart Kids, 2001.

Smith, Ryan. *Ships from Start to Finish*. Farmington Hills, Mich.: Blackbirch, 2005.

Stewart, David. *Avoid Sailing on the Titanic*. Jonesville, Mich.: Book House, 2002.

Wilkinson, Philip. *The World of Ships*. New York: Kingfisher, 2005.

Wilson, Patrick. *Navigation and Signaling*. Broomall, Penn.: Mason Crest, 2002.

For some extra fun, dive into some of these fictional tales about life at sea:

Jackson, Melanie. *The Mask on the Cruise Ship*. Custer, Wash.: Orca Books, 2004.

Leonhardt, Alice. *Case of the High Seas Secret*. New York: Harper and Collins, 2001.

Marsh, Carole. *The Cruise Ship Mystery*. Peachtree City, Ga.: Gallopade International, 2006.

Osborne, Mary Pope. *Tonight on the Titanic*. New York: Random House, 1999.

Shearer, Alex. *Sea Legs*. New York: Simon and Schuster, 2006.

🗣 WITH THE EXPERTS

Cruise Lines International Association
910 SE 17th Street, Suite 400
Fort Lauderdale, FL 33316-2968
http://www.cruising.org

NorthWest Cruiseship Association
100-1111 West Hastings Street
Vancouver, British Columbia V6E 2J3
http://nwcruiseship.org

Shipbuilders Council of America
1455 F Street NW, Suite 225
Washington, DC 20005
http://www.shipbuilders.org

GET ACQUAINTED

Susan Dziama, Cruise Director

CAREER PATH

CHILDHOOD ASPIRATION:
To be a heart surgeon.

FIRST JOB: Working at a fast-food restaurant.

CURRENT JOB: Youth activities manager on the *Explorer of the Sea* cruise liner.

HEARTFELT AMBITIONS

When Susan Dziama first started thinking about her future career, she put her desire to help people together with her interest in science. That led to the idea of becoming a heart surgeon. When she went to college, she even minored in biology, which is a good premed choice.

Her major was secondary education with an emphasis in physical education. And that major turned out to be a great fit for the job she landed just one week after she graduated. No, it wasn't a job as a heart surgeon. It wasn't even a job as a high school physical education teacher.

It was a job that Dziama applied for after seeing a sign on campus advertising for summer work on a cruise line. Since Dziama graduated in May and schoolteachers typically

don't start teaching until August or September, she had an empty summer looming ahead and decided to fill it with some adventure. After a couple rounds of interviews, Dziama was offered a job managing youth activities aboard a Royal Caribbean cruise ship. Talk about perfect timing! The offer came in one day before she graduated. Within a week, all her belongings were safely stowed at her parents' house, and she was on her way to New York for training.

YOU MEAN I GET PAID FOR THIS?

Dziama's job is cruise director for the younger set. She and her staff of 14 entertain between 100 and 800 children and teens every week for five months straight. Their days begin at 9:00 A.M. and end at 2:00 A.M. (yes, that's A.M.!). Activities are planned for four different age groups—the little folks who are 3 to 5, the kids who are 6 to 8, the big kids who are 9 to 12, and the 13- to 17-year-old teens. The daily schedule is jam-packed with what Dziama calls "camp at sea." There are adventures in science, computer art projects, theme nights, dinner at the Johnny Rocket Diner, and dancing and entertainment at the teen nightclub (that's where the late nights come in).

It's all done with one goal in mind—everybody's got to have fun! Little did Dziama realize when she signed her first contract that she'd be having as much fun as the kids. She says paydays are just icing on the cake.

HOME SWEET BERTH

Dziama is a manager, so she gets her own cabin on board the ship where she lives for 10 months out of the year. She says it's like living on a floating city. The crew has their own mess hall, nightclub, gym, and activities manager—all the comforts of home at sea.

Every year, Dziama gets two months of vacation time. She generally spends a couple of weeks visiting her family and the rest gallivanting to new places she wants to explore. So far, these travels have included London, Paris, and San Francisco.

SETTING SAIL

Dziama's first assignment was aboard the cruise ship Voyager, which regularly set sail for such exotic ports as Haiti, Jamaica, Panama, and Bermuda. She was recently reassigned to the brand-new *Explorer*, which docks in Miami en route to hot spots such as San Juan, St. Thomas, and Nassau. What a life!

Detective

SHORTCUTS

GO find out if your local police station offers tours or special programs for young people.

READ a good mystery and see if you can figure out who committed the crime.

TRY deciphering the hidden codes found online at http://www.thunk.com.

SKILL SET

✔ TALKING

✔ COMPUTERS

✔ ADVENTURE

WHAT IS A DETECTIVE?

Whether it's a murder or a lost child, a bank robbery or insurance fraud, a terrorist threat or business espionage, tax evasion or contraband drugs, you can bet that there's a detective on the case. The law boils down to this—crime does not pay. It is a detective's job to track down the culprits and bring them to justice.

There are lots of different kinds of detectives including police officers working in small rural communities, private investigators, and special agents for the Federal Bureau of Investigation (FBI). Police detectives may work to solve a specific type of crime such as homicide. Highway police officers often must investigate the causes of automobile accidents and other incidents. Fire departments have special investigators who determine the cause of fires. This type of work is usually assigned to experienced police officers with special training.

The federal government also employs several different kinds of detectives. Most widely known is the FBI. These agents may investigate terrorism, bank robberies, organized crime, and kidnappings, and then will often work in cooperation with local law enforcement agencies to solve a case. Other government detectives include Immigration and Naturalization Service agents, U.S. marshals, and special agents for the Bureau of Alcohol, Tobacco, Firearms, and

Explosives (ATF), the Internal Revenue Service, the Secret Service, and U.S. Border Patrol.

Private investigators work on a large variety of cases for individuals or corporations. These cases may be centered around corporate espionage, shoplifting prevention, electronic surveillance, finding family members, or other kinds of problems involving families. Another type of private investigator, a bail bondsman, or bounty hunter, will help to find those people who have skipped bail and bring them in to stand trial. Often, a corporation will employ a full-time security expert, another type of detective, to be sure the company's ideas, employees, and products are safe.

Along with detectives who work the streets solving crimes through investigations, interrogations, and other methods, there are detectives who work in laboratories looking for clues in some of the most unusual places. They include the doctors, called coroners, who perform autopsies as they look for clues about how a person died. Also included are the forensic scientists or criminologists who look for clues in the evidence gathered by detectives. They use such things as fingerprints, fiber analysis, and DNA tests in their work. Another kind of detective is a profiler, who specializes in the psychological side of things, studying criminal behavior and giving other detectives ideas about the kinds of people capable of committing certain types of crimes.

For all of these people, the work can be dangerous, time-consuming, and extremely stressful. A detective never knows what a new day will bring and must be ready for anything. Detective work seldom involves gunfights and high-speed car chases like you see on TV. Instead, there is a lot of careful, routine work that involves gathering clues, sifting through evidence, talking to people, checking out computer information, searching through records in courthouses and libraries, and testing and retesting theories and ideas. It might mean sitting on surveillance detail for long periods of time just watching and waiting for someone to do something. Paperwork, and lots of it, is another part of the job.

Detective work requires training and experience. Sometimes, as in many police departments, experience counts as much as or more than education, so detectives often rise through the ranks of the department. Other kinds of detective work, especially those involving the federal government and those involving complicated scientific skills, do require college degrees. For instance, if you want to work for the FBI, you must have a college degree plus a law or accounting degree, or you must have work or language experience to compensate. All jobs generally require some on-the-job training as well, which can range from a few weeks to a few months. Passing written and practical tests is also necessary to become licensed.

Detective work can be an ideal choice for the adventurous type with a strong sense of right and wrong. Curiosity, good people skills, and creative and analytical thinking skills also come in handy in this line of work.

☞ TRY IT OUT

LET YOUR FINGERS DO THE TALKING
Find out more about how fingerprinting is done and how it helps detectives fight crime at these Web sites:

- ❀ http://www.cyberbee.com/whodunnit/fp.html
- ❀ http://www.fbi.gov/fbi/kids.htm

⚲ http://pbskids.org/zoom/activities/sci/fingerprints
.html

Use the information you find there to make fingerprint
cards of all your family members or a couple of friends. You'll
need an ink pad or washable magic markers, and index cards
labeled with each person's name. Use Scotch tape to "lift"
fingerprints from around the house and see if you can match
the prints with the person they belong to.

THE CASE OF THE MISSING BOOK

Here's a case that's sure to need your detective skills. Ask
your school librarian if there are any books that have mysteri-
ously disappeared. If your school is like most, there will be a
few. Try using your detective skills to track it down. Who had
it last? Do they still have it? Where was it last seen? Can you
get it back? Record notes about each step of your investigation and the final results in a small, spiral notebook.

✔ CHECK IT OUT

🖱 ON THE WEB

ARMCHAIR DETECTIVES

There's nothing quite like a good mystery story. Along with
some great classics such as the Hardy Boys mysteries and
Nancy Drew adventures, there are now some fun ways to
solve the crimes online. Look for clues at Web sites such as:

⚲ Kids Love a Mystery at http:www.kidsloveamystery
.com
⚲ Mystery Net for Kids at http://kids.mysterynet.com
⚲ The Case of Grandpa's Painting at http://www.eduweb
.com/pintura
⚲ History Detective Kids at http://pbskids.org/
historydetectives
⚲ Crime Scene Investigation at http://www.cyberbee
.com/whodunnit/crimescene.html

ONLINE INVESTIGATIONS

Here are just a few Web sites of interest to young detectives. Do some investigating on your own and you're sure to find more.

- ☆ ATF for Kids at http://www.atf.treas.gov/kids
- ☆ FBI for Kids at http://www.fbi.gov/fbikids.htm
- ☆ Frequently Asked Questions by Kids at http://www .treas.gov/usss/kids_faq.shtml
- ☆ U.S. Marshals for Kids at http://www.usmarshals.gov/ usmsforkids

📚 AT THE LIBRARY

THROW THE BOOK AT CRIME

There's nothing like a good mystery to give you goose bumps. Curl up with some of these mystery favorites and see if you can figure out whodunit.

Classics like the Nancy Drew series by Carolyn Keene (New York: Grosset and Dunlap), the Hardy Boys series by Franklin W. Dixon (New York: Grosset & Dunlap), and *The Boxcar Children* by Gertrude Chandler Warner (New York: Albert Whitman and Company) are great places to start your sleuthing.

Other fun and mysterious reads include:

Fitzhugh, Louis. *Harriet the Spy.* New York: Yearling, 2001.
Koningsburg, E.L. *From the Mixed-Up Files of Mrs. Basil E. Frankweiler.* New York: Aladdin, 1998.
Marsh, Carole: *Around the World in 80 Mysteries* (series). Peachtree City, Ga.: Gallopade. 2006.
Sobol, Donald. *Encyclopedia Brown: Boy Detective.* New York: Yearling, 1985.

WITH THE EXPERTS

Bureau of Alcohol, Tobacco, Firearms and Explosives
650 Massachusetts Avenue NW, Room 8290
Washington, DC 20221-3796
http://www.atf.treas.gov

Federal Bureau of Investigation
J. Edgar Hoover Building
935 Pennsylvania Avenue, NW
Washington, DC 20535-0001
http://www.fbi.gov

National Council of Investigation and Security Services
7501 Sparrows Point Boulevard
Baltimore, MD 21219-1927
http://www.nciss.com

United States Border Patrol Supervisors' Association
539 Telegraph Canyon Road
P.M.B. #656
Chula Vista, CA 91910-6497
http://www.bpsups.org

United States Customs and Border Protection
1300 Pennsylvania Avenue NW
Washington, DC 20229-0001
http://www.cbp.gov/xp/cgov/home.xml

United States Department of Justice
Drug Enforcement Administration
Mailstop: AES
2401 Jefferson Davis Highway
Alexandria, VA 22301-1055
http://www.usdoj.gov/dea

United States Marshals Service
Employment and Compensation Division
600 Army Navy Drive
Arlington, VA 22202-4221
http://www.usmarshals.gov

United States Secret Service
Personnel Division
245 Murray Drive, Building 410
Washington, DC 20223
http://www.treas.gov/usss

GET ACQUAINTED

Tom Goodpaster,
Private Investigator

CAREER PATH

CHILDHOOD AJPIRATION:
To be a spy.

FIRST JOB: Dishwasher for a restaurant.

CURRENT JOB: Licensed private detective and owner of Blue Heron Investigations.

SMILE AND SAY "CHEEJE!"

Tom Goodpaster started out wanting to be a photographer, so he studied photography for two years and earned an associate of applied arts degree in photography. Later, he wanted to become a police officer, so he went back to school for two years and earned an associate's degree in law enforcement. Both areas of interest came together while he was waiting to get hired as a police officer; he met a man who had once been a private detective. His stories sounded interesting, and so Goodpaster applied for a job as a private detective. His future boss liked that he knew how to use a camera and gave Goodpaster a chance to work for his private investigation firm for the summer. That was nearly 20 years ago and he's been doing it ever since!

MORE THAN ONE WAY TO INVESTIGATE A CASE

Many private detectives specialize in just one kind of investigation and perform that kind of investigation day after day. Goodpaster used to be one of them. Today, though, he is what's referred to as a *generalist* and conducts many different kinds of investigations. He may run a background investigation on someone, conduct surveillance of a person to see what they do throughout the day or night, locate someone who doesn't want to be found, install a hidden camera to catch a thief, or find electronic listening devices (bugs) that a spy or snoop has installed in a home or business.

Goodpaster has investigated everything from bank robberies and murders to the whereabouts of a stolen dog. He's tracked down fugitives, found runaway and abducted children, and caught people committing criminal acts right on tape.

He says that no two days are exactly alike so there is no "typical day." One day he might get up at 4:00 A.M. to begin surveillance. On another day, he might not get home until 4:00 A.M.! Once, he went to work thinking he'd be home for dinner but found himself working a thousand miles from home and didn't get home for a week. Another case that he thought would take just two days to complete took nine days to wrap up. Since he'd only brought along enough clean clothes for a couple of days, he wound up doing laundry in a laundromat in a foreign country.

A typical week for Goodpaster involves working "in the field" for about two to three days. The rest of the week is spent in the office writing reports, consulting with people, and billing clients.

PROBLEM-SOLVING, STRESS RELIEF, AND PAPERWORK

Goodpaster says that the best part of his job is helping people solve problems. By the time a person calls a private detective like him for help, that person has given up all hope of being able to solve the problem on his or her own. He also likes the variety that the job provides. Many times, especially if he's conducting surveillance, he has no idea what he'll be doing or where he'll be going until the person he's watching goes there! This aspect of the job certainly keeps things interesting.

On the other hand, being a private detective can be stressful. Sometimes there are places he'd rather not go and people he'd just as soon not meet. Since, unlike police officers, most private investigators work alone, he doesn't have a partner or radio dispatcher to rely on if things go wrong and he finds himself in an unsafe situation. Since nobody else knows where he's located or who he's with most of the time, he finds that he must always stay aware of his surroundings and never forget that there's usually at least one person who doesn't want him there.

There is also paperwork to contend with. Just because Goodpaster solved the case doesn't mean that his job is done. The case isn't closed until he writes a detailed report regarding his findings, bills the client for his work, and continues to talk to potential new clients who want to hire him for the next case.

ADVICE FOR FUTURE DETECTIVES
Goodpaster says that he's known a lot of private detectives, and even though none of them had the exact same background or training, they all had one thing in common: a clean record. None of them had ever been convicted of stealing anything, destroying someone's property, or doing illegal drugs. If they had, they would have been barred for life from ever becoming a private detective. Goodpaster says the best advice he can give future detectives and private investigators is this: Stay out of trouble, learn how to write a good report, and never stop asking yourself "why?"

Diplomat

SHORTCUTS

GO to United Nations online at http://www.unol.org.

READ *Inside A U.S. Embassy: How the Foreign Service Works for America* by Shawn Dorman (Washington, D.C.: American Foreign Service Association, 2001).

TRY taking lots of writing, public speaking, and foreign language courses.

WHAT IS A DIPLOMAT?

Choose to pursue a career as a diplomat and you choose much more than a job; it's a way of life that often requires commitment, dedication, and personal sacrifice. A diplomat represents the United States and promotes its values and interests around the world—whenever and wherever they are needed.

Diplomats, or foreign service officers, as they are also called, work at the State Department in Washington, D.C., and in embassies and consulates in almost every recognized nation in the world. The mission of these embassies and consulates is multifaceted and includes national security, assisting and protecting Americans living and traveling abroad, and advancing American policy interests.

There's no law that says a diplomat must have a college degree, but most of them have earned not only undergraduate college degrees but advanced degrees as well. English, economics, political science, and international studies all provide a good educational foundation for diplomatic work. Mastery of another language is also helpful, if not downright essential. Look beyond the basic Spanish and French into languages less commonly studied in U.S. schools, such as Chinese, Russian, and Arabic.

Armed with the proper credentials and training, prospective diplomats are required to pass the foreign service exam—a tough test on such things as foreign affairs, English, writing, and management skills. Applicants who pass the exam move on through intensive background checks and an oral assessment of their temperament, people skills, and ability to interpret and report on events. Applicants who make it through this round are placed on a list of eligible candidates and are contacted when a position becomes available. Please note that of the more than 10,000 applicants who take the test every year, only about 300 are ever posted as diplomats. However, there are other kinds of positions available within the realm of the State Department, so keep your options open.

Those lucky few who make the final cut are hired as junior officers and spend several weeks at the National Foreign Affairs Training Center before being sent on their first overseas assignment. They sometimes receive foreign language instruction as well as an education in the history, customs, and culture of their assigned country. Overseas assignments last from about 18 months to 4 years. After that, a diplomat may be brought stateside for a tour or sent to another country.

Diplomats specialize in one of five specific areas or "cones." Cones are assigned or selected early in a diplomat's career and are more or less followed throughout a diplomat's career path.

Officers in **administrative affairs** are responsible for the daily operations of embassies and consulates. Their duties include overseeing budgeting, personnel, communications, and security.

Consular affairs officers help U.S. citizens who are traveling or living in their host country. They issue passports, register births and marriages of U.S. citizens, and keep locator information of Americans so they can be found and evacuated in case of an emergency. They also provide assistance for foreigners wanting to enter the United States.

Economic affairs diplomats collect, analyze, and report information relative to foreign economies. They must have an excellent understanding of the U.S. economy and the economy of their host nation.

Political affairs officers keep up with political events and conditions in their host country and report the same to the State Department. They also deliver official messages from the U.S. government to government officials in their host country.

Public diplomacy officers communicate between the United States and their host country. They promote U.S. interests and policies as well as attempt to give their host government an understanding of what America is all about.

These five areas are fairly diverse, but the State Department has identified skills and knowledge that are basic requirements for all diplomats. They include the following: proper English usage; knowledge of U.S. society, culture, history, government, political systems, and the Constitution; and knowledge of world geography, international affairs, world political and social issues, basic accounting, statistics and mathematics, management, communication, and economics.

Junior officers or diplomats have a probationary period of four years. During this time, they are expected to satisfy foreign language requirements. If they pass muster, they are tenured, which means they can't be fired without a good reason. After receiving tenure, they can compete with other diplomats for choice assignments and promotions.

Anywhere, anytime is the creed of our nation's diplomats. Diplomats go where they are needed—even if it isn't exactly a dream location. Serving in developing nations with rough and sometimes dangerous living conditions is just as likely a scenario—if not more so—as black-tie state dinners with the Queen of England.

Diplomats perform a valuable service to their country. It can be an exciting and challenging career choice—even noble at times. Globe-trotters who want to see the world and make a difference in world affairs may find the diplomatic corps a career to consider.

☞ TRY IT OUT

REPORTING FOR DUTY!

Get online and go to a list of U.S. embassies at http://usembassy.state.gov. Link to an embassy and learn everything you can about the economic and political conditions in a particular country. You can get more information about that country by using the CIA's World Factbook at http://www.cia.gov/cia/publications/factbook/index.html. Gather as much information as possible and then write a detailed report about the economy and politics of your country. Where are the hot spots? What are the big issues the country is grappling with? What is the United States doing to help?

DIPLOMACY IN ACTION

Diplomacy is a famous board game by Avalon Hills. You can probably find it at your local game and hobby shop. It is a strategy game that will allow you to test your aptitude for diplomacy as you try to take over the world. There are many groups who play online. You can get familiar with the online version at http://www.diplom.org.

✔ CHECK IT OUT

 ON THE WEB

VIRTUAL EMBASSIES

The world's embassies are where diplomacy happens every day. Visit some (or all!) of them online at these Web sites:

- ☼ Visit Web sites of all the U.S. embassies in the world at http://usembassy.state.gov
- ☼ Visit Web sites of all the world embassies located in Washington, D.C., at http://www.embassy.org/embassies
- ☼ Visit Web sites of virtually every embassy in the world at http://www.embassyworld.com/embassy/directory.htm

Make sure to stop by these embassy Web sites that are designed just for kids:

- ☼ Embassy of France for Kids at http://www.ambafrance-us.org/kids
- ☼ Israel Embassy for Kids at http://www.israelemb.org/kids

DIPLOMATIC RELATIONS

Find out more about how the United States deals with its international friends and foes at:

- ☼ U.S. State Department for Youth at http://future.state.gov
- ☼ Central Intelligence Agency (CIA) for Kids at https://www.cia.gov/cia/ciakids/index.shtml
- ☼ European Union Fun and Games at http://www.eurunion.org/infores/teaching/Young/fun.htm
- ☼ Visit the Global Schoolhouse at http://www.globalschoolnet.org/GSH/index.html

AT THE LIBRARY

GLOBAL READS

Here's a list of books about diplomacy and international relations to look for at your local library or bookstore. You may also want to look for resources about a specific place in the world.

Cunningham, Kevin. *Condoleezza Rice: U.S. Secretary of State*. Chanhussen, Minn.: Child's World, 2005.

Gunderson, Cary Gideon. *When Diplomacy Fails*. Edina, Minn.: Abdo & Daughters Publishing, 2003.

Miller, Debra. *U.S. Involvement in the Middle East: Inciting Conflict*. Farmington Hills, Mich.: Lucent, 2004.

Nakaya, Andrea. *Does the World Hate the United States?* Farmington Hills, Mich.: Greenhaven, 2004.

Ruffin, David C. *The Duties and Responsibilities of the Secretary of State*. New York: PowerKids Press, 2005.

Tapper, Suzanne Cloud. *America as a World Power: From the Spanish-American War to Today*. Berkeley Heights, N.J.: Enslow, 2007.

Watson, Susan. *Making Global Connections*. Mankato, Minn.: Smart Apple Media, 2003.

WITH THE EXPERTS

American Foreign Service Association
2101 E Street NW
Washington, DC 20037-2990
http://www.afsa.org

Associates of the American Foreign Service Worldwide
5555 Columbia Pike, Suite 208
Arlington, VA 22204-3117
http://www.aafsw.org

Council on Foreign Relations
1779 Massachusetts Avenue NW
Washington, DC 20036-2109
http://www.cfr.org

Executive Council on Foreign Diplomacy
818 Connecticut Avenue NW, 12th Floor
Washington, DC 20006-2702

GET ACQUAINTED

Chuck Hunter, Diplomat

CAREER PATH

CHILDHOOD ASPIRATION:
To be an author.

FIRST JOB: Cleaning up a clothing store and painting houses.

CURRENT JOB: Congressional Liaison for the U.S. State Department Bureau of Legislative Affairs.

A DEBATABLE CAREER CHOICE

Chuck Hunter is a self-professed bookworm and has been one since he was a child. Back then he loved to read history and biographies, and he was especially fascinated to learn about the presidents.

Hunter also discovered an affinity for foreign languages when he got the opportunity to start studying French in the sixth grade. He enjoyed the sound of putting new words together. In fact, he enjoyed it so much that he continued to study the language throughout high school and even pursued a double major in French and government in college.

Both of these factors played a role in Hunter's career choice, but there was one additional detail that tipped the scales in favor of diplomacy: he got involved in his high school's speech and debate team. He discovered he was pretty good at it, and his coach encouraged Hunter to think about putting all of these interests together as a foreign service officer.

SEEING (AND SERVING) THE WORLD

As soon as Hunter graduated from college, he jumped through all the hoops required to apply for a job with the State Department, and he passed every hurdle. However, while he was waiting for his background check to clear, he was offered a fellowship to attend graduate school at Stanford. It was an offer too good to refuse. Five years later, with a doctoral degree in French and the humanities firmly in hand, Hunter once again applied for a job as a diplomat. Once accepted, he chose an assignment in the public affairs cone.

Now, after more than 10 years of diplomatic service, Hunter has spent time in Algeria, Egypt, Tunisia, Oman, Jerusalem, and Washington, D.C. His diplomatic career started with a year of language training in Washington, D.C., followed by tours in Egypt and Algeria, where he served as assistant public affairs officer. The Algerian tour was abbreviated when civil unrest broke out and 50 percent of the Americans working at the embassy were evacuated. After a brief stint in D.C., Hunter was back for another year of language study in Tunisia and a three-year posting as public affairs officer (PAO) in Oman. Stateside duties have included serving in the Near Eastern Affairs office, with responsibilities to keep tabs on things in Amman, Beirut, Jerusalem, Tel Aviv, and Damascus, and director of press relations for the State Department's Bureau of Public Affairs. His current position is head of the State Department's liaison office on Capitol Hill.

So far, Algeria is the only post where his proficiency in French has been called upon. But that's the result of a carefully calculated decision Hunter made early on. Looking at the options, Hunter realized that the Middle East is an important place in diplomatic terms. He felt certain that work in that region was likely to "really matter" in world affairs. So he took the plunge and volunteered to specialize in Arabic (one of four languages that the State Department considers super hard—the others being Chinese, Japanese, and Korean). It's a decision Hunter has yet to regret as he continues to view events in the Middle East as pivotal to the rest of the world. Even the possibility of serving in Iraq, which he has volunteered to do, looks at least as exciting as it might be scary.

DIPLOMATIC NEGOTIATIONS

Hunter has a few suggestions for young people hoping for a diplomatic future. Although learning another language is an obvious suggestion, Hunter says it's more than just learning words; he's found that learning to understand the language of another culture is a huge step toward understanding the people and making sense of a system that is different from your own. He also thinks it's important to learn about life outside the United States. As citizens of the world's super-power, Americans have so much—a good standard of living and good government—that it's easy to get wrapped up in our own little world, according to Hunter. Awareness of other peoples and places can help cultivate the openness and toler-ance necessary to contribute to and live in a world of peace, stability, and security.

Oh, and one more thing while you're at it. How about ask-ing your parents to get you a passport for your next birth-day? It's not that expensive, it's valid for 10 years, and who knows when you might need it!

Event Planner

SKILL SET

✔ TRAVEL

✔ TALKING

✔ MATH

WHAT IS AN EVENT PLANNER?

Meetings make the business world go around. Event planners make sure all those meetings go well—whether it's a convention, seminar, sales meeting, product introduction, or celebration.

Event and meeting planners work in different ways to get the job done. Some are on the staff of a large corporation. Their primary responsibility is to plan meetings and special events for various departments in the company. Anything from arranging an incentive trip to Hawaii to planning a training seminar to hosting the company holiday party might fall under a corporate meeting planner's job description.

Other meeting planners work for professional associations and may be responsible for planning a huge annual convention involving thousands of members, hundreds of special workshop sessions and exhibitors, and all kinds of special events. Marketing the convention to association members and keeping track of registration information may come with the territory as well.

Another type of event planner works for (or owns) an event planning company. Some of these companies specialize in arranging incentive trips to wonderful locations for clients who want to reward their staff or colleagues, while others focus on planning fund-raising galas for charity organizations or other types of special events.

The one thing that all meeting planners have in common is details—and plenty of them. It starts with lots of questions: What type of event does the client have in mind? Where will it be held? How many people do they expect to attend? What is the project budget? And on and on the questions go.

As questions get answered, a theme often starts to emerge, and then the real planning begins. The meeting planner plans down to the last detail. After developing a budget, the first big decision is deciding where the event will take place. This is where the travel comes in. Event planners frequently make trips to check out potential event locations. They might look at several different hotels or convention centers to see which can best meet the needs of the event.

Food is an important part of most meetings and events, so menu selection is another big decision. Depending on the kind of event, planners may line up speakers, special training sessions, recreational activities, and entertainment.

They also arrange for any necessary audiovisual, lighting, or sound equipment. Then there are the decorators, florists, and security considerations to be determined. Don't forget that out-of-town guests may need transportation and hotel arrangements!

No matter what type of event, meeting and event planners can expect to arrive early and leave late. Early arrival assures that everything is ready to roll when the event begins. The mark of a well-planned event is one that runs smoothly. Good meeting planners make their jobs look easy by making sure that even the smallest details are handled without a glitch. After the event is over, there is still work to do. Supervising clean-up and paying suppliers are part of the follow-up process, as is some sort of evaluation or final report to the client.

Event planners tend to be very creative and well organized. They have excellent contacts and communications skills. Since meeting planners also work with budgets, a head for figures is also required.

It used to be that most meeting and event planners learned the tricks of the trade on the job, while working as an assistant to an experienced planner. Some still do. Increasingly, however, meeting and event planners are finding that a degree in hospitality or event or meeting management gives them the edge they need in this competitive industry. Earning certificates in programs offered by Meeting Planners International or the International Special Events Society provides some extra clout on the résumé, too. Both of these credentials require experience in the field and successful completion of a written exam.

☞ TRY IT OUT

JOIN THE CLUB

Get your start by planning meetings and events at your school or place of worship. There are probably dozens of clubs that have weekly or monthly meetings and special events. Join one and volunteer to help plan an upcoming meeting. Be sure to get involved with the committee that plans the school dances, too!

PARTY!

Get your parents' permission to host a party at home. Make a checklist of all the details you have to arrange, such as invitations, food, drinks, decorations, and entertainment. Try to come up with a unique theme for your event and find creative ways to carry it out. After your party, get feedback from your guests about what they liked and disliked. Make notes throughout the process so that your next party will be easier to plan.

PARTY 2!

Imagine you are a professional meeting planner and you have been hired by your favorite professional sports team to plan a huge party to celebrate their latest win. The whole team and their families, the media, and lots of important people will be there. They want to make a huge splash and money is no object. Let your imagination run wild as you plan an awesome event complete with great food, fabulous decorations, and top-notch entertainment. Sketch out details of your plans in a notebook. Don't forget to include a knock-out invitation so no one in their right mind will want to miss this party!

✔ CHECK IT OUT

🖱 ON THE WEB
VIRTUAL MEETING PLANNER

Find ideas and inspiration for your next kid-friendly event at some of these Web sites:

- ☼ Kids' Holiday Party Plans at http://childparenting.about .com/od/kidsholidayparties
- ☼ Kids Parties Connection at http://www.kidsparties.com
- ☼ Kids' Parties Planning Guide at http://www.party411 .com/kids.html
- ☼ Party Planning Links at http://www.suite101.com/ links.cfm/party_planning

💡 Party Planning Themes and Ideas for Kids at http://
entertaining.about.com/od/kidsparties

 **AT THE LIBRARY**

PARTY IN A BOOK

Get the lowdown on giving the best parties in town in books like:

Bonner, Lori. *Putting on a Party.* Layton, Utah: Gibbs Smith,
2004.

Brian, Sarah Jane. *Party Secrets: Who to Invite, Most-Loved
Munchies, Must-Dance Music, and Foolproof Fun.* Middleton, Wisc.: Pleasant Company, 2003.

Busby, Cylin. *Pajama Party Under Cover.* New York: Grosset &
Dunlap, 2003.

Ross, Kathy. *Best Birthday Parties Ever: A Kid's Do-It-Yourself
Guide.* Minneapolis: Millbrook Press, 1999.

Snooze-a-palooza!: More Than 100 Slumber Party Ideas.
Middleton, Wisc.: Pleasant Company, 2005.

🗣 WITH THE EXPERTS

Alliance of Meeting Management Consultants
3890 Clubland Drive
Marietta, GA 30068-4008
http://www.ammc.org

International Special Events Society
401 North Michigan Avenue
Chicago, IL 60611-4267
http://www.ises.com

International Society of Meeting Planners
1224 North Nokomis NE
Alexandria, MN 56308-5072
http://www.iami.org/ISMP/home.cfm

Meeting Professionals International
3030 Lyndon B. Johnson Freeway, Suite 1700
Dallas, TX 75234-2759
http://www.mpiweb.org

The Professional Convention Management Association
2301 South Lake Shore Drive, Suite 1001
Chicago, IL 60616-1419
http://www.pcma.org

GET ACQUAINTED

Shelley Matheny, Event Planner

CAREER PATH

CHILDHOOD ASPIRATION: To work with children and travel.

FIRST JOB: Folding towels in her aunt's beauty salon.

CURRENT JOB: President and CEO of KidsAlong, Inc.

THE ACCIDENTAL MEETING PLANNER

Shelley Matheny didn't plan on becoming an event planner; she sort of got thrown into it after graduating from college with a business degree. She answered an ad for an administrative assistant job that, unknown to her at the time, had been placed by one of the world's largest incentive travel agencies. She got the job, loved it, and within two weeks was actually planning events. A couple of years later, she moved on to a smaller company where she was responsible for planning events from start to finish, which proved to be a great way to learn even more about the event planning process.

When that company went out of business, she was hired to join the special events and conferences staff of a large corporation. At that time, the company's in-house event planning division was known as the best in the business. It was such a large operation that it included an entire department to cover airline arrangements, another department to handle conference registrations, and eight meeting planners. This job turned out to be Matheny's dream come true. She traveled all over the world managing 8 to 10 different conferences.

HAVE CHILDREN, WILL TRAVEL

From the very first job, Matheny knew she wanted to be a meeting planner. But after giving birth to her second child, Matheny needed a job with more flexibility. Starting her own meeting planning business—where she could pick and choose when and where her time was spent—was the next logical step in her career path.

She found just the right twist for her business when a large company asked her to put together a program for the 150 children who would be accompanying their parents to a conference in Hawaii. Matheny put together a winning children's program complete with adventure hikes, tennis workshops, hula lessons, painting coconuts, treasure hunts, and making leis. When Matheny realized that she'd had just as much fun as the kids, she knew she was on to something for her own business.

That's when KidsAlong, Inc. was born. The company specializes in providing imaginative children's programs for meetings and conferences. Matheny says that her job requires all the meeting skills that she's acquired along the way—and then some. Matheny's business handles about 25 events each year, involving anywhere from 30 to 1,500 children in places all over the world. American cities such as Palm Springs, San Francisco, New York City, Hilton Head, and New Orleans have been home to some of Matheny's programs, while Canada, Mexico, Austria, and Italy are some of the far-flung locations her work has taken her. No matter where the meeting is held, no two events are ever the same. Each program is custom designed and extra special.

THE RIGHT STUFF

Matheny doesn't mean to brag or anything, but she thinks she's got a great job. She says that it probably never occurs to a lot of kids that there is a real career out there called *meeting planner*. But there is, and Matheny heartily recommends it.

She says that many schools even offer training programs just for meeting planners. As for Matheny, she learned how to do it by actually doing it. But she did take the time to complete the requirements to obtain a Certified Meeting Planner credential. It's a designation that indicates to clients that she knows what she's doing and shows a certain commitment to her profession.

If you'd like to know about more Matheny's really cool job, you can visit her Web site at http://www.kidsalong.com.

Expedition Leader

SHORTCUTS

SKILL SET

✔ **ADVENTURE**

✔ **ANIMALS & NATURE**

✔ **SPORTS**

GO lead a group of friends on a nature hike.

READ *The Lewis and Clark Expedition* by Christin Ditchfield (Danbury, Conn.: Children's Press, 2006).

TRY climbing an indoor climbing wall at a recreation center near you.

WHAT IS AN EXPEDITION LEADER?

This career is all about discovery—discovery of new places, new people, and new experiences. Some expeditions involve physical daring—a trip to Nepal to climb Mount Everest, a scenic bike tour to see the leaves in New England, sea kayaking in Baja, or a challenging hike through a national park. Others involve special interests such as fashion, art, or history. People go on expeditions to take on new challenges, discover new worlds, or learn something they didn't know about themselves.

The leader of an expedition is responsible for pretty much everything that makes an expedition so exciting. Managing the basics like travel arrangements, food, and lodging are one part of the job. Another part is planning a schedule of events that will provide a memorable experience for each customer. The expedition leader must carefully attend to every detail. Routes and transportation must be exact, activities must be planned, arrangements must be made, employees must be trained, food and supplies must be sufficient, equipment must be in good repair, emergency supplies must be on hand, and so on. In cases where expeditions are held off the beaten path, such as a jungle safari or white-water rafting trip, there won't be a convenience store or fast food restaurants on every corner. (There might not even be a corner!) What you carry in your backpack is what you've got to survive on, so good planning pays off.

Generally speaking, an expedition leader must be physically fit. If backcountry skiing is the purpose of the expedition, the

leader must be an awfully good skier. The same thing goes for scuba diving, fishing, whatever the type of the expedition. Expedition leaders have to know their stuff.

Quite often, physical rigor isn't the only focus of expeditions. Many revolve around learning about a wide range of topics. Whether it's antiques or marine biology, team members expect the leader to be an expert in the field—or close to it.

People skills are a must to lead and motivate all kinds of people through all kinds of challenging situations. Problem-solving skills won't hurt, either, since there are always new situations to work out.

There isn't a school that you can attend to become an expedition leader. People drawn into this profession usually have a passion for a certain activity or place. In one sense, they are teachers, using the world as their classroom. In another, they are true adventurers, stretching the limits of themselves and others.

 TRY IT OUT

BACKYARD TREK

You don't have to go far for an expedition. Take a couple of friends on a trek to your own backyard. Get your parents' permission and gather supplies to camp out overnight. You'll need food, shelter, a source of light, and so on. Make sure to plan a full schedule of challenging events. Put together an obstacle course or schedule some Olympic-style competitive events and any other activities you think your friends would enjoy—safely. Maybe some scientific experiments or stargazing would fit the bill. Don't forget the ghost stories!

LOST AND FOUND

Here's an activity that's sure to build your courage and confidence. Ask an experienced adult to take you on a trek in the woods. Pack your backpack with some snacks, some water, a trail map, and a compass. Take a look at the map and decide where you want to go, and then tuck the map away in your backpack. See if you can rely on the compass for directions and your wits for guidance to get you where you want to go. Look at the map only if you must to keep from getting lost. Keep a travel log of your hike to record where you go and what you see.

ON THE TRAIL WITH LEWIS AND CLARK

When it comes to exciting expeditions, it's hard to beat the adventures of American explorers Lewis and Clark. Find out more about their historic exploits by going online and using the Yahooligans search engine (http://www.yahooligans.com) to run a search using the words "Lewis and Clark." Use the information you find there to create a timeline that describes their famous journey.

# ✔ CHECK IT OUT

🖱 ON THE WEB

TOP THIS IF YOU CAN

- 💡 Find brief biographies of men and women who have explored the earth and skies at http://www.enchanted learning.com/explorers.
- 💡 See if you can pass fun quizzes about early explorers at http://www.mce.k12tn.net/explorers/explorers_start.htm.
- 💡 Link to information about explorers past and present at http://www.kidinfo.com/American_History/Explorers .html.

☀ Get acquainted with some women famous for their adventures at http://www.infoplease.com/spot/whmbios13.html.

☀ Join in the adventures of some virtual explorers at http://www.virtualexplorers.org.

☀ Enjoy a weekend getaway online at http://www.pbs.org/weekendexplorer.

 AT THE LIBRARY

BACKYARD TREK

Find ideas for some kid-friendly adventures in books such as:

Hayhurst, Chris. *Bike Trekking: Have Fun, Be Smart.* New York: Rosen, 2000.

Peterson's. *Summer Opportunities for Kids and Teenagers.* Lawrenceville, N.J.: Peterson's, 2006.

Rhatigan, Joe. *The Kids' Guide to Nature Adventures: 80 Great Activities for Exploring the Outdoors.* Asheville, N.C.: Lark Books, 2003.

Wilson, Jef. *Hiking for Fun!* Minneapolis: Compass Point, 2006.

Winner, Cherie. *Kids Gone Campin': The Young Campers Guide to Having More Fun Outdoors.* Alpharetta, Ga.: Creative Publications, 2006.

ARMCHAIR EXPLORERS!

Make mountain-top treks, dive in the deepest seas, and visit the North Pole—all from the comfort of your coziest chair with this fascinating series of books:

Chapman, Simon. *Explorers Wanted in the Desert.* New York: Little Brown, 2006.

———. *Explorers Wanted in the Himalayas.* New York: Little Brown, 2005.

———. *Explorers Wanted in the Jungle.* New York: Little Brown, 2005.

———. *Explorers Wanted at the North Pole.* New York: Little Brown, 2005.

———. *Explorers Wanted on Safari.* New York: Little Brown, 2005.
———. *Explorers Wanted on South Sea Islands.* New York: Little Brown, 2005.
———. *Explorers Wanted Under the Sea.* New York: Little Brown, 2005.

WITH THE EXPERTS

Boy Scouts of America
PO Box 152079
Irving, TX 75015-2079
http://www.scouting.org

Earthwatch Institute
Three Clocktower Place
Suite 100, Box 75
Maynard, MA 01754-2574
http://www.earthwatch.org

Girl Scouts of America
420 Fifth Avenue
New York, NY 10018-2798
http://www.girlscouts.org

National Geographic Society
1145 17th Street NW
Washington, DC 20036-4688
http://www.nationalgeographic
  .com

GET ACQUAINTED

Martha Culp,
Expedition Leader

CAREER PATH

CHILDHOOD ASPIRATION:
To be a veterinarian.

FIRST JOB: Babysitting and weeding people's yards.

CURRENT JOB President and director of Inside Out, Inc., which provides adventure expeditions for kids.

INQUIRING MIND

When Martha Culp was growing up, she loved being outdoors. She enjoyed hiking, camping, and splashing in streams. As a child, she often collected water samples at nearby streams and ponds. Then she'd go home to look at things under her microscope.

Now that she's an adult, her company, Inside Out, Inc., is a natural fit. She gets to work with kids, which she loves, and her work involves one adventure after another. She plans expeditions that go all over the world. It's an incredible job! You can find out more at Culp's Web site at http://www .insideout-inc.com. They also do a lot of team-building events and hands-on, outdoor science activities.

CHALLENGE BY CHOICE

One thing Culp tries to do with each expedition is provide opportunities for kids to make challenging choices and to develop new skills. The idea is to gently nudge them to accomplish things they never thought they could do. Whether it's rock climbing or rushing down a river in a kayak, kids break through their own barriers at their own speed. Depending on the situation, this part of Culp's job can either be really fun or really hard.

Sometimes it's tough to stay quiet when students are trying to figure out how to overcome a challenge. The easy way out would be for Culp to just tell them what to do, but that would defeat the entire purpose of the challenge. She's learned to bide her time and watch for each person to find his or her own solution to the problem.

CHART THE COURSE

Planning and more planning is what Culp does before each trip. Logistics is a big deal when you are trying to get a group of people and a bunch of equipment from one place to another. Food, equipment, and other supplies must all be packed ahead of time.

Every piece of gear must be inspected to make sure it's in working order. Tents have to be tight, sleeping bags clean and rolled, and ropes ready. "There's nothing worse than waking up in the middle of the night with rain dripping on your face because there's a small hole in the tent," Culp says. Her job is to make sure that doesn't happen.

SAFETY IN NUMBERS

Safety is also a big concern for Culp. Teamwork is one way that Culp makes sure that her expeditions are as safe as possible. For instance, when rock climbing, one person climbs a sheer wall of rock, while another secures the rope that keeps the climber safe. Each team member must be able to trust the others to do their part.

Culp says that, a while ago, she took an expedition into the woods with a group of kids who had never been camping before. They didn't know how to pitch a tent or build a fire or cook their food. No one knew anyone else, so communication didn't come easily. On the expedition, the group began to learn new things together. They really jelled as a team and began to interact with each other. Culp says, "By the end of the trip, they really didn't need me. It was fun to watch the different personalities come together to do the jobs that needed to be done."

NEVER A DULL MOMENT

This job is full of diverse and interesting things to do. There isn't a typical day or a typical program or a typical group. It's all different. Culp finds herself morphing from one area to the next as she works out logistics, checks gear, orders food, sets up activities, and figures out van pick-up points and campsites.

"There's nothing boring about this job," she says. "Each moment is filled with a discovery of some new thing in the universe, a new way of doing things, a personal limit that is pushed. I challenge myself, whether it's working on gear maintenance, taking a long hike, or doing the office work. That's part of discovering more about me."

Fashion/Commercial Model

SHORTCUTS

SKILL SET

✔ ART

✔ TALKING

✔ ADVENTURE

GO online to see some popular fashions at http://www.gap.com.

READ some popular fashion magazines to see what's hot and what's not.

TRY getting involved with your local community theater.

WHAT IS A FASHION/COMMERCIAL MODEL?

You'll probably see the results of what models do for a living before you go to sleep tonight. They are everywhere! Pass a billboard on the way home from school—there they are. Watch TV—there they are. Read the newspaper or flip through a magazine. Yep, they are there too. Models are the people featured in commercials and advertisements to sell all kinds of products—not just clothes, either. Models pitch everything from Apple computers to Zale's jewelry.

When you think model, the first thing that may come to mind is fashion model—those beautiful girls and guys who walk the runways for designers creating a glamorous image for the season's new fashions. In actuality, there are many different avenues open to people interested in modeling. Fashion models most often get the spotlight for their role looking beautiful in front of a camera; their work can take them to exotic locales around the globe for just the right setting or scenery. Their job demands that they rigorously maintain their appearance to meet industry requirements.

But models also work in artist's studios, posing for drawings and paintings, and professional conferences and exhibitions where they help present products and generate publicity. If you're interested in modeling, the first thing to do is decide which branch of the business is right for you.

To be a fashion model generally requires that you have a certain "look" and meet some pretty strict height and weight requirements. Some people think if you aren't drop-dead gorgeous, you'll never make it as a model, but that's not true. At least, not exactly. You may never grace the cover of the hottest fashion magazines unless you have the "look," but that doesn't mean there aren't other opportunities for people who look like—for lack of a better way of saying it—"real people."

Commercial modeling is part acting and part modeling. These models can be male or female, young or old, short or tall, skinny or not so skinny. The job may require assuming a certain role such as a housewife going gaga over the new laundry detergent or a teen hip-hopping around in the latest cargo jeans for a television commercial. It may involve being photographed wearing fashions from a local department store for a newspaper ad. Some commercial models are known for special kinds of assignments such as hand modeling, where the only thing photographed is their hands—usually wearing an exquisite piece of jewelry or advertising nail polish or another type of hand-care product.

There is no formal education required to be a commercial model. However, classes are often available through modeling agencies or finishing schools that provide training in some of the finer points of commercial modeling. Models are often represented by agents who scout out modeling assignments for them. Many models work in the industry only part time. They may be full-time students or have another job that helps pay the bills and fill in off-camera time.

Models sometimes market themselves by putting together a group of pictures, called a composite, showing them in different settings and situations, wearing different types of clothes. Their composite is circulated among advertising agencies that evaluate it for the types of projects they are working on. If the model fits the criteria for a project, he or she could land an assignment. Other times models will go to an audition—a *go-see*—where digital pictures are taken of the models in specific kinds of settings. This allows the photographer, the ad agency representatives, and the client to choose models that best meet the criteria they are looking for.

An actual photo shoot is full of action. Preparation may include makeup, clothes, hair styling, and rehearsal—all of which comes before the camera starts rolling. After that, it's not just a simple matter of smiling and saying "cheese." It can be hard work to get just the look the client is after. It can take dozens of poses and hundreds of shots.

After the shoot, there's still work to be done, mostly paperwork to be filled out: releases, contract vouchers, thank-you notes, invoices, and other items.

The work can be a bit glamorous at times, but mostly it's just hard work. It can get boring sitting around waiting for photographers to set up equipment and adjust lights. But it can also be lots of fun, involving travel to unusual places and providing a chance to make new friends.

One of the most important parts of being a model is staying true to your own goals, standards, and values. Sometimes it can be easy to get swept away in the excitement of it all. Commercial modeling isn't about being thin and beautiful or becoming a star. It's about discovering the beauty that is already inside you and letting it shine. Be careful about falling for those "let me make you a star overnight" scams, and always involve your parents in any modeling assignments you accept before you're 18. Set your sights on where you want to be and go for it!

 TRY IT OUT

SAY CHEESE!
Save up your money for a digital or a disposable camera (there are some nifty new versions). Get a friend or two together, some of your favorite outfits, and some interesting props. Take turns snapping photos of each other using a variety of emotions and going for different looks.

Use these photos to put together a composite. Mind you, this is just for practice. If you really decide to go after some commercial modeling assignments, you will need professional-quality photographs in your composite. However, this is a good way to get an idea of what the process is like.

SCOUT SOME TALENT
Turn the tables for this activity. Instead of being the model, take on the role of the agent or client. First, thumb through a magazine and pick a few products to sell—maybe toothpaste, a sophisticated new perfume, a sports car, or a minivan. Cut out pictures of just the product and attach each one to a separate sheet of paper. Now go through the magazines again

looking for photographs of the types of models who you think match each product. Think about what kind of model will sell each product best. Would it be a man or a woman? Should the model be old or young, short or tall, beautiful or ordinary? What kinds of clothes and props would help set the right mood? Clip any photos you like and attach them to the appropriate page. Look at the clothing and accessories. Try cutting out just the clothing and matching it to other pictures of models to see if you can find the best look or fit for that item. This will give you an idea of how models are selected for various projects.

BE CAREFUL OUT THERE!

Do not—repeat, do not—even consider a career as a commercial model until you read an article called "If You've Got the Look . . . Look Out!" found online at http://fashion.about .com/cs/models/l/blmodelscam.htm. The article is courtesy of the U.S. Federal Trade Commission and provides some very frank cautions about the modeling industry. Read it and make two checklists: one for dos and one for don'ts. Make sure that your career decision is based on facts and good advice, not fantasy and scams.

✔ CHECK IT OUT

ON THE WEB

FASHION FUN AND GAMES

- ☼ Design a heavenly wardrobe for the fashion angels at http://www.fashionangels.com/site.html
- ☼ Check out some of the latest fashion trends for students at Newshour fashion issue at http://www.pbs .org/newshour/on2/fashion.html
- ☼ Help Claire get ready at http://www.claires.com/ getting_ready.asp
- ☼ Find links to all kinds of online dress-up games at http://www.i-dressup.com

📚 AT THE LIBRARY

MODELING 101

Find out more about the modeling profession in books like:

Ferguson. *Discovering Careers for Your Future: Fashion.* New York: Ferguson, 2004.

Mauro, Lucia. *Careers for Fashion Plates and Other Trendsetters.* New York: McGraw-Hill, 2002.

Maze, Stephanie. *I Want to be a Fashion Designer.* New York: Harcourt, 2000.

O'Donnell, Kerri. *Careers in Modeling.* New York: Rosen Publishing Group, 2001.

And for some tips on snazzing up your own personal style, try:

Kauchak, Therese. *Real Beauty: 101 Ways to Feel Good About You.* Middleton, Wisc.: Pleasant Company, 2004.

Smith, Allison Chandler. *The Girls' World Book of Bath & Beauty: Fresh Ideas & Fun Recipes for Hair, Skin, Nails, & More.* Asheville, N.C.: Lark Books, 2004.

THE FASHION STORY

Get up to speed with fashion past and present with the *Fashions of a Decade* series (New York: Facts On File, 2006). There are titles from every decade from the 1920s through the 1990s. For extra fun and inspiration, make a fashion notebook to start recording fashion trends in the 2000s.

🗣 WITH THE EXPERTS

Barbizon School of New York
16 Penn Plaza, Suite 1205
New York, NY 10001
http://www.modelingschools.com

Candy Ford Group
1354 Hancock Street
Quincy, MA 02115-5109
http://www.candyford.com

Ford Models Inc.
111 Fifth Avenue
New York, NY 10003-1005
http://www.fordmodels.com/main.cfm

IMG Models
304 Park Avenue South, 12th Floor
New York, NY 10010-4301
http://www.imgmodels.com

GET ACQUAINTED

Aaron Marcus,
Commercial Model

CAREER PATH

CHILDHOOD ASPIRATION: To be a major league baseball player.

FIRST JOB: Working in his father's wholesale men's clothing store.

CURRENT JOB: Commercial model, actor, author, lecturer, and publisher.

MUSICIAN TO MODEL

Aaron Marcus was a musician first and played in a band with his brother for six years. It was fun while it lasted, but he eventually opted out to go to school to become a physical therapist.

Once in school, however, he discovered a little problem. He needed a job to support himself while he was studying. He started to do a bit of commercial modeling just to pay the bills. He set some goals before he started, giving himself one year to earn enough money to finish his education.

As it turned out, Marcus really liked modeling. He liked it so much, in fact, that he decided to try it full time. Since 1986, he has worked more than 1,050 times on various modeling assignments.

A JOB YOU CAN GET INTO

According to Marcus, there's a special thrill of being on a job that's out of the ordinary. He finds that, especially when the emotional angle is tough, he has to totally immerse himself in the set, taking on the character he is supposed to represent. When he really gets into it, he's oblivious to anything else.

He spends time the night before getting ready and practicing, being sure that he has all the necessary props. He won't just show up and expect everything to go smoothly. Marcus spends a good chunk of time preparing, including getting that all-important good night's sleep.

"When everything goes well, when I'm totally prepared and am feeling all the right emotions, then the photographer and I get into a sort of dance—the rhythm of the shoot that makes everything just click." For Marcus, that's the best.

HO-HUM

Sometimes Marcus has to drive a very long distance to get to a shoot, which he doesn't mind too much. It's all the waiting on the set that can get to be a bit of a drag. To pass the time, he brings along a book to read while he's waiting. It could be a new novel, an acting book, marketing information about modeling, newsletters, or company magazines. He's learned never to go anywhere without something to read. While on set, he also likes to observe and learn new things about the industry. This greatly helps him with producing "The Tear Sheet," his newsletter about modeling and acting.

HELPFUL ADVICE

Marcus' advice to you is to do your homework before you start. He's had years of experience, thoroughly researched the modeling industry, and found there are a few things that are important to check out early. These include: getting wonderful commercial photos done and putting together your composite, finding agents, making contacts, getting work

on your own, getting the documents you need to have, and knowing when your parents should be involved. He advises that when you take a class, you should audit a couple of sessions first to see what it's like. It can save you in the long run. Marcus was so concerned that people would get hooked into stuff they shouldn't that he wrote a book about it. You can find out more at his Web site at http://www.howtomodel .com or find out if your library or local bookstore has a copy of Marcus' book, *How to Become a Successful Commercial Model* (Baltimore: Marcus Institute of Commercial Modeling, 2005). You can also read two chapters for free and order a copy of his book (for a fee) at his Web site.

Firefighter

SHORTCUTS

GO visit a nearby fire station.

READ *Virtual Apprentice: Firefighter* by Diane Lindsey Reeves (New York: Ferguson, 2007).

TRY running up and down several flights of stairs, wearing a backpack full of books.

WHAT IS A FIREFIGHTER?

Thank goodness for firefighters! If you've ever been in a fire, an accident, or other emergency, you know how important their work is. Sirens wailing and lights flashing, firefighters show up when bad things happen.

Whether it's a fire, an accident, a medical emergency, or some other type of catastrophe, firefighters are trained to handle almost any situation that comes their way. The training starts with several months of intensive firefighting preparation and it really never stops. As long as people keep finding new ways to get into trouble, firefighters need to keep learning ways to help them.

Before the training starts, however, potential firefighters have to meet some fairly rigorous requirements, including passing a written test, a physical test of strength and endurance, and a medical examination. Applicants must be at least 18 years old and have a high school education or equivalent. A college degree isn't required, but those who have a college degree or have taken some community college courses in fire science have a better chance of being hired. Often competition is heavy for the few firefighter slots available.

Physical fitness is critical to performing well in an emergency. Fires aren't easy to fight. Before the flames die down, a firefighter may have to handle large hoses that carry heavily pressurized water, run up flights of stairs, climb ladders, and rescue people or pets. Even though those tasks are hard

enough all by themselves, firefighters must do them while wearing heavy protective gear and equipment.

Fighting fires isn't the only thing that firefighters do. Hazardous materials, floods, earthquakes, terrorism, medical emergencies, and accidents also get the trucks rolling from the firehouse. In addition, firefighters are often called upon to rescue people and animals that need help—including cats stuck in trees.

Day or night, when the call comes, firefighters answer immediately. That's why firefighters generally work in 24-hour shifts and sometimes sleep at the fire station at least a couple of nights a week. But if the alarm rings at 3 A.M., it is up and at 'em. If it rings at dinnertime, dinner has to wait.

Some firefighters also visit schools and provide programs on safety and fire prevention. They perform inspections on older buildings and work with builders to make sure that plans for new structures comply with fire codes. They may also work in conjunction with law enforcement officers to protect both people and property.

Other firefighters, called *hotshots* or *smoke jumpers*, work with the U.S. Forest Service to prevent and put out forest fires as well as rescue hikers and climbers. Sometimes you'll see sto-

ries about their heroic efforts on TV during the hot summer months when forest fires often rage out of control.

Fires at refineries, gas stations, chemical plants, or paint stores are especially dangerous and require firefighters with special training and equipment. In these cases, a hazardous materials truck goes out on the call, staffed by firefighters who have special hazmat training.

Any kind of firefighting is dangerous work. That's why firefighters take safety very seriously. Injuries can occur from smoke inhalation, floors collapsing, explosive gases and chemicals, and other dangers. Good training not only helps firefighters do their job, but it also keeps them safe. Many times it can mean the difference between life and death.

Firefighting isn't a way to get rich quick by any means. But sometimes being a hero is worth a lot more than money. If you've ever been rescued by one, you know that hero is the only word that adequately describes a firefighter.

👉 TRY IT OUT

TELL THE SAFETY STORY

Get together with a couple of your friends and write a skit on fire safety for little kids. Can you come up with a hit skit? Ask your teacher to help you find a way to present your program to other kids in your school or a nearby preschool. Use costumes, puppets, posters, or other memorable activities to teach children about fire safety.

FIRST AID FAST

Firefighters and emergency medical technicians (EMT) often work side by side in emergency situations. Increasing numbers of firefighters also earn EMT credentials. In either case, a working knowledge of first aid comes in handy for emergency professionals as well as for kids like you.

Use the following resources to find "what to do if" tips for a variety of common first aid situations (nosebleed, bee sting,

etc.). Write step-by-step advice for each situation on a separate three-by-five-inch index card and keep your collection handy for dealing with life's little emergencies.

💡 Boelts, Maribeth. *Kids to the Rescue: First Aid Techniques for Kids.* Seattle: Parenting Press, 2003.
💡 Gale, Karen Buhler. *Kids Guide to First Aid: All About Bruises, Burns, Stings, Sprains, and Other Ouches.* Nashville, Tenn.: Williamson: 2002.

Also check the following Web sites for information:

💡 http://kidshealth.org/parent/firstaid_safe/index.html
💡 http://www.mayoclinic.com/health/FirstAidIndex/FirstAidIndex

✔ CHECK IT OUT

🖱 ON THE WEB
HOME, SAFE HOME
Pick up a home inspection checklist from your local fire station or go online to http://www.homesafetycouncil.org/safety%5Fguide/sg_fire_p001.pdf. Use the checklist to inpect your home for fire safety. How do you rate? Be sure to test your smoke alarms. Locate all the exits in your house. In a fire, would you be able to get out in time? Pick a place away from the house for everyone to meet in case of a fire. Hold a fire drill for your family.

ONLINE FIREFIGHTING
You can learn a lot online about fighting fires and preventing them. Here are a few Web sites to try:

💡 Find out if you could survive this simulated fire situation at http://www.survivealive.org
💡 U.S. Fire Administration for Kids at http://usfa.fema.gov/kids/flash.shtm

- ☼ National Fire Prevention Association Risk Watch for Kids Only at http//:www.nfpa.org/riskwatch/kids.html
- ☼ Staying Alive Kid's Zone at http://www.stayingalive .ca/kids_zone.html
- ☼ Find out more about smoke jumpers at http://www .smokejumpers.com
- ☼ Visit a Web site where real firefighters go for the latest information at http://www.firefighting.org

AT THE LIBRARY
FIREFIGHTING BY THE BOOK

Abraham, Philip. *Firefighter.* New York: Children's Press, 2003.

Beyer, Mark. *Smokejumpers: Life Fighting Fires.* New York: Rosen Publishing Group, 2001.

Ganci, Chris. *Chief: The Life of Peter J. Ganci, A New York City Firefighter.* New York: Orchard, 2003.

Gorrell, Gena K. *Catching Fire: The Story of Firefighting.* Plattsburgh, N.Y.: Tundra Books, 1999.

Gottschalk, Jack. *Firefighting.* New York: DK Publishing, 2002.

Kelley, Alison Turnbull. *First to Arrive: Firefighters at Ground Zero.* New York: Chelsea House Publications, 2002.

Maze, Stephanie. *I Want To Be A Firefighter.* New York: Raintree, 1999.

Wheeler, Jill C. *Firefighters.* Minneapolis: Checkerboard Books, 2002.

WITH THE EXPERTS

International Association of Fire Chiefs
4025 Fair Ridge Drive
Suite 300
Fairfax, VA 22033-2868
http://www.iafc.org

International Association of Fire Fighters
1750 New York Avenue NW
Washington, DC 20006-5395
http://www.iaff.org

National Association of State Fire Marshals
1319 F Street NW, Suite 301
Washington, DC 20004-1140
http://www.firemarshals.org

National Fire Protection Association
One Batterymarch Park
Quincy, MA 02169-7471
http://www.nfpa.org

National Interagency Fire Center
3833 South Development Avenue
Boise, ID 83705-5354
http://www.nifc.gov

National Smokejumper Association
PO Box 1022
Lakeside, MT 59922-1022
http://www.smokejumpers.com

National Volunteer Fire Council
1050 17th Street NW, Suite 490
Washington, DC 20036-5519
http://www.nvfc.org

GET ACQUAINTED

Tracee Kelly, Firefighter

CAREER PATH

CHILDHOOD ASPIRATION:
To be a teacher.

FIRST JOB: Babysitting.

CURRENT JOB: Firefighter
and paramedic.

FROM ALASKA TO ARIZONA

Tracee Kelly grew up in Alaska and wanted to be a teacher. But she remembers being fascinated by the firefighters who came to her school to talk about safety. However, she assumed it wasn't a job for a woman.

By the time she graduated from high school, she was all set to go after a career in medicine. She went all the way through college and earned a premed degree.

Then she took some time off from school to work as a "hotshot" firefighter for the U.S. Forest Service in Arizona, and she loved it. Kelly ended up spending two summers digging fire breaks and helping to contain forest fires. She hiked with other hotshots and camped out, doing work that was very challenging physically. Great meals, along with the opportunity to make new friends and learn about fires, almost made up for not being able to shower and having to sleep on the ground.

THE BOOT

The experience in Arizona changed Kelly's life. She decided to use what medical training she already had as a firefighter instead of going on to become a doctor. She was accepted into a firefighter academy where she went through fire fighting boot camp, a challenging training experience. Even now on the job, she must continue to get 30 hours of additional training each month in areas of firefighting, emergency medical procedures, and hazardous materials.

Kelly also spends at least an hour a day, when she is on duty and off, working out. "All of us are very athletic," she says. "I have to pull my weight here. That means being able to pull hose, carry heavy packs, and run up stairs quickly." Being in shape can mean the difference between life and death in some situations. She keeps fit so she never lets the rest of her team down.

FIREHOUSE FAMILY

Firefighters often become an extended family. During 24-hour shifts, Kelly and four firefighters work, live, eat, and relax together. They take turns with such things as meal preparation and cleanup. "The neat thing is," Kelly says, "if you cook, you don't have to clean up." Dinners especially are lively, with lots of teasing, and occasional harmless pranks on one another.

Just like real families, when the going gets tough, this family sticks together. If one member becomes injured or sick for a long period of time, it's not unusual for others to cover extra shifts so he or she doesn't miss a paycheck.

Firefighters often help with on-the-job problems and personal ones as well. "We're there for each other, just as a family would be," she says. "We truly are our brother's keeper, both on the job and off. We depend upon each other, especially when people's lives are at stake. We have to function as a team, a family, In order to get things done."

LOTS OF LAUGHS

Firefighting boots and hat isn't the only uniform that Kelly wears. Quite often, she also wears a clown costume and goes to schools with other firefighters to talk about fire safety. As a clown, she can reach the younger kids with important, life-saving information and have a roaring good time while she's at it.

MORE THAN WORTH IT

For Kelly, the most exciting part of her job is being able to help others. She tries to stay very aware of the fact that, when firefighters are called, it is often because of bad news. People are scared and in danger. Sometimes she is able to help turn tragedy into triumph.

Knowing her work can make a difference gives Kelly the courage to do what she needs to do. Every time she hears the bell in the fire station, jumps into her gear, and takes off on a fire truck with sirens wailing and lights flashing, Kelly knows she is on her way to save lives.

Foreign Correspondent

SHORTCUTS

GO to the video store and rent the Alfred Hitchcock film *Foreign Correspondent.*

READ the work of foreign correspondents in the world news section of a major newspaper or newsmagazine.

TRY doing volunteer work on the school newspaper.

WHAT IS A FOREIGN CORRESPONDENT?

Foreign correspondents are journalists who report news and events from other countries. Their jobs involve travel, excitement, danger, intrigue, and historic events.

Foreign correspondents report for newspapers, magazines, cable and television networks, radio broadcasts, news wires, and online news services. They are first and foremost reporters, and their work is similar in many ways to the work of counterparts who work in the United States. The biggest difference is that foreign correspondents do their reporting from other parts of the world.

Like other journalists, foreign correspondents go after newsworthy stories and sometimes have to go to great lengths to get them. They collect information through research, interviews, and contacts. They analyze this information and write stories that are clear, factual, and free from personal bias. Their stories cover all the bases of who, what, where, when, why, and how.

With foreign correspondents often covering volatile parts of the world, there's no room for mistakes. Facts must be checked and rechecked. Not only are the journalists' reputations on the line, but, quite often, important aspects of our nation's international relations hinge on accurate reporting of current events; foreign correspondents are our nation's eyes and ears in other parts of the world.

Getting the inside scoop depends on being in the right place, at the right time, with the right contacts. Some reporters are assigned to cover the foreign desk of a particular country or region of the world, which allows for on-the-spot coverage as significant events take place. Other correspondents move from place to place, following big, breaking news stories.

It is not uncommon for foreign correspondents to find themselves in war zones. They often get to see history unfold before their eyes. Many have literally put their lives in danger to get the story. More than one foreign correspondent has lost his or her life in the line of duty.

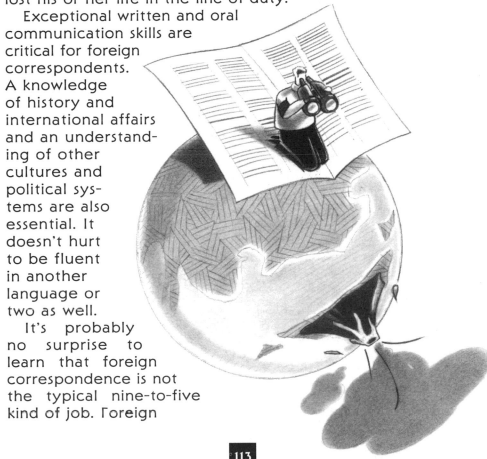

Exceptional written and oral communication skills are critical for foreign correspondents. A knowledge of history and international affairs and an understanding of other cultures and political systems are also essential. It doesn't hurt to be fluent in another language or two as well.

It's probably no surprise to learn that foreign correspondence is not the typical nine-to-five kind of job. Foreign correspondents work when and where news is breaking, even if that means round-the-clock coverage of a big story. They tend to keep their bags packed in case they have to get to a story on a moment's notice. Deadlines can create tremendous pressure. However, quiet news days offer opportunities for sniffing out leads, cultivating contacts, and enjoying other places in the world.

Foreign correspondents need a college degree in a subject such as journalism, English, communications, political science, or history. It is very uncommon for someone to be hired as a foreign correspondent right out of school. Most earn their stripes working at smaller papers; then move to larger, national news organizations; and eventually land jobs as foreign correspondents after lots of hard work.

Foreign correspondents keep the world informed about what's happening in other places. Their work helps shape our perception of the world, and it is often instrumental in shaping foreign policy and effecting change. Whether it's some sort of social injustice, a natural disaster, or all-out war, foreign correspondents are on the spot to get the word out.

 **TRY IT OUT**

THE WRITE STUFF
Start getting the valuable writing experience you'll need as a foreign correspondent by writing for your school newspaper. Also, contact the editor of your hometown paper and see if they accept articles from students. You may be able to submit stories about sports and other school activities for publication. Don't forget to clip (cut out and save) your published articles so you can start your portfolio.

SNIFF OUT A STORY
Sniff out an international event on the Web. Research and gather facts from several sources and write a story.

Reuters at http://www.reuters.com is a good source for the latest international news.

Make a chart with a column for each of these news sources:

- http://abcnews.go.com
- http://www.cbsnews.com
- http://www.cnn.com
- http://www.foxnews.com
- http://www.msnbc.msn.com

List the international headlines at each Web site and compare how each source covered the story. Do they report similar facts? Do they approach the stories from different angles? Can you spot any bias or personal opinions in any of the stories?

✔ CHECK IT OUT

🖱 ON THE WEB
READ ALL ABOUT IT

Use your favorite Internet search engine, such as http//:www .yahoo.com or http://www.google.com, to find out more about the fascinating work of Martha Gellhorn. She was a foreign correspondent for more than 60 years and covered the Spanish Civil War, World War II, and Vietnam. Other famous foreign correspondents—past and present—to investigate include Nellie Bly, Margaret Fuller, Ernie Pyle, and Christiane Amanpour.

GET THE SCOOP

Sniff out some noteworthy information at these Web sites:

- Make some newsworthy connections at http://www .nytimes.com/learning/students.
- Go around the world in 72 days with investigative reporter Nellie Bly at http://www.pbs.org/wgbh/ amex/world.
- See what it's like to cover news in a war zone at http://www.newseum.org/warstories/index.htm.
- Write headline news with a little help from some British journalists at http://www.headlinehistory.co.uk/ swf/main_launcher.htm.

☀ Visit the kids' newsroom at http://www
  .kidsnewsroom.org.

☀ Catch the latest news at Time for Kids at http://www
  .timeforkids.com/TFK.

📚 AT THE LIBRARY

AN ARMCHAIR ADVENTURE

Find out more about what it's like to be a journalist in books
such as:

Bowman-Kruhm, Mary. *Day in the Life of a Newspaper
  Reporter*. New York: Rosen, 2001.

Bonnice, Sherry. *Journalist*. Broomall, Pa.: Mason Crest Publishers,
  2003.

Careers In Focus: Journalism. New York: Ferguson, 2005.

Cupp, Dave and Cecilia Minden. *Television Reporters*. Chanhassen, Minn.: Child's World, 2006.

Englart, Mindi. *How Do I Become a TV Reporter?* Farmington
  Hills, Mich.: Blackbirch Press, 2003.

———. *Made in the U.S.A.: Newspapers*. Farmington Hills,
  Mich.: Blackbirch Press, 2001.

Somervill, Barbara A. *Ida Tarbell: Pioneer Investigative
  Reporter*. Greensboro, N.C.: Morgan Reynolds, 2002.

Sullivan, George. *Journalists at Risk: Reporting America's Wars*.
  New York: 21st Century, 2004.

Just for fun, read some of the titles in the Get Real series
published by HarperCollins. The fictional books are written by
well-known journalist Linda Ellerbee (you may have seen her
on *Nick News* on the Nickelodeon channel) and features girl
reporter Casey Smith.

🗣 WITH THE EXPERTS

International Federation of Journalists
IPC-Residence Palace, Bloc C
Rue de la Loi 155
B-1040 Brussels
Belgium
http://www.ifj.org

National Association of Broadcasters
1771 N Street NW
Washington, DC 20036-2800
http://www.nab.org

National Press Club
529 14th Street NW, 13th Floor
Washington, DC 20045-1000
http://npc.press.org

The Newspaper Guild
501 Third Street NW, 6th Floor
Washington, DC 20001-2797
http://www.newsguild.org

The Overseas Press Club of America
40 West 45th Street
New York, NY 10036-4202
http://www.opcofamerica.org

Society of Professional Journalists
3909 North Meridian Street
Indianapolis, IN 46208-4011
http://www.spj.org

GET ACQUAINTED

Alison Smale,
Foreign Correspondent

CAREER PATH

CHILDHOOD ASPIRATION:
To be an archaeologist.

FIRST JOB: Usher at a local movie theater.

CURRENT JOB: Managing editor of the *International Herald Tribune*, an overseas partner of the *New York Times*.

A FAMILY TRADITION

Alison Smale grew up in England, where her father was a financial reporter. She thought his job seemed nice enough since it allowed him to go places and meet interesting people. As a child, she had always thought she wanted to be an archaeologist. But when she turned 16 and everyone else seemed to have a plan for their lives, it was a logical leap to announce journalism as her goal. And why not? It didn't require as much patience as being an archaeologist did!

Smale's college majors were German and political science and included one year of study in Germany. After graduating, Smale decided she wanted to see America—not the America tourists saw during three weeks aboard a Greyhound bus, but the real America. The opportunity to do just that presented itself in the form of a full scholarship to study for a master's degree at Stanford University.

Her studies in the United States proved to be a wonderful experience and eventually led to her first job as a foreign correspondent. Part of her training involved an internship with United Press International (UPI), an international newswire service, in Germany and London. After she graduated, she was offered the chance to return to Germany to run the Bonn office—quite an accomplishment for such a young reporter.

THE WORLD ACCORDING TO SMALE

While in Germany, she covered such historic events as Iran's release of U.S. hostages, the royal wedding of Prince Charles and the late Princess Diana, and issues related to the Cold War as they played out in East Germany. She also accepted a job with the Associated Press (AP), another worldwide news service.

This new allegiance led to a coveted job in Moscow. Long fascinated by the Soviet Union and affairs in Eastern Europe, Smale found herself right in the middle of some of the most pivotal times in that region's recent history. She had a first-hand look at what it was like to live in Communist countries, and she was there to see the struggles of many of those countries to regain their freedom.

A RUSSIAN ROMANCE

It was while she was in Russia that she met and fell in love with a Russian pianist and composer—much to the chagrin of the KGB. Russia's infamous secret police didn't favor the relationship. After all, Smale was a foreign correspondent, suspicious in and of itself. The couple responded by being as open as possible about their relationship, despite pressures from the KGB.

Things really came to a head when the couple married and Smale was assigned to a new job in Vienna. At first, the Russian government refused to grant Smale's husband a visa so that he could go with her. Knowing that she had a choice to make, Smale opted to work within the system instead of making a major fuss about it in international headlines. Her subtle approach won out in the end—her husband received a visa—and Smale says she learned a valuable lesson in the process. She says she discovered that, if you really believe in something or love someone, you can always find a way to make things work out.

NEXT STOP—VIENNA

Smale's next assignment was in Vienna. She was AP's bureau chief for Eastern Europe and led a staff of some 70 reporters. It was a heady time to be in this part of the world as communism fell in country after country. War erupted in Yugoslavia during Smale's Eastern Europe assignment. She said it was horrifying to see a wonderful country deteriorate into mindless destruction as neighbor fought neighbor while the rest of the world tried to pretend nothing was wrong. Smale found that the only way to fight the fear was to work, work, work, and to try not to think about the awful things she was covering in her stories.

While she's seen her share of danger and excitement as a journalist, Smale says she learned always to have a way out before she put herself in harm's way. She'd take necessary precautions such as wearing a flak jacket and helmet, but she says there's really only one way to keep yourself out of danger and that is to think. Yes, she's had a few close calls and even experienced a sniper attack in Sarajevo (no one in the press car was injured), but she always seemed to manage to get out in time.

A CHANGE OF PACE

For several years Smale was an assistant foreign editor for the *New York Times*. She is responsible for putting out the weekend editions of the foreign affairs section of this major newspaper. While a desk in a New York City newsroom is a bit removed from the front line of a war zone, Smale says it represents a natural progression in her career and gave her more time for her husband and young daughter (born just a month after the Bosnian war broke out).

Now Smale is managing editor of the *International Herald Tribune*, an overseas partner of the *New York Times*. Smale has responsibilities on both sides of the Atlantic Ocean again and has resumed her globe-trotting ways.

International Businessperson

SHORTCUTS

GO to a big department store and read the labels on various products to see where they were made.

READ the business section of a major newspaper to find out what's happening in the world of business.

TRY getting to know a foreign exchange student at your school to learn about a different culture.

WHAT IS AN INTERNATIONAL BUSINESSPERSON?

It's a small world, and thanks to innovations in transportation, communications, and technology, the world is becoming one big marketplace. Never before have there been so many ways to see the world at work.

Virtually any job you can do in your homeland, you can do abroad. Increasing numbers of American companies have branch offices in overseas locations (and vice versa), which means that someone has to do the same jobs there that get done here, and everything from janitor to CEO is up for grabs. International jobs require actually relocating to a new place to live and working in another culture.

Another kind of international business opportunity involves being based in one country and making occasional or frequent trips to other countries. Thousands of businesspeople function in this way—whether it's a publisher working with an overseas printer or a banker investing in overseas businesses. This type of situation often offers the best of both worlds— the excitement of global travel with all the comforts of home just a flight away.

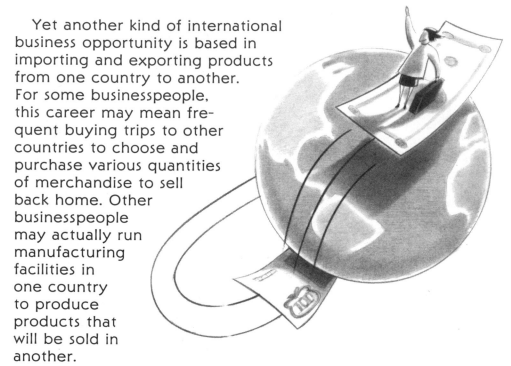

Yet another kind of international business opportunity is based in importing and exporting products from one country to another. For some businesspeople, this career may mean frequent buying trips to other countries to choose and purchase various quantities of merchandise to sell back home. Other businesspeople may actually run manufacturing facilities in one country to produce products that will be sold in another.

While the educational route necessary to prepare for a career in international business is as varied as the available occupations, most successful globe-trotters share a few common traits, such as good analytical and organizational skills, strong oral and written communication skills, computer literacy, fluency in languages, and effective interpersonal skills. It also helps to be self-starting, adaptable, and flexible.

Beyond that, there are many avenues for training. Foreign language fluency (in at least one language) and an MBA will equip you for some of the most lucrative international jobs. You could try undergraduate work in economics, business, marketing, or in a specialized field such as textiles or manufacturing. Or, if you are absolutely certain of your goals, get a degree in international business. A good program will cover subjects such as accounting, marketing, finance, and management.

By its very nature, international business tends to require quite a bit of globe-trotting. Getting from your home state, wherever it may be, to Europe, Asia, or Latin America is no small feat. Take this little quiz to see if you've got what it takes to be a world traveler:

- Bad hair days become the norm when traveling in countries that don't accommodate your electrical personal grooming appliances. Can you deal with it? Yes or No.
- Sushi? Kimchi? No matter how unusual or exotic the native food gets, just bring it on! Yes or No.
- There's nothing like a good night's sleep aboard a roaring 747. Sound like a dream to you? Yes or No.
- Finding your way in a place where few others speak your language—would that challenge you in a positive way? Yes or No.
- Adjusting your habits and manners to those considered acceptable in your host country—is that something you can deal with comfortably? Yes or No.

Those questions touch on some of the issues that international businesspeople encounter every day. Although they may seem insignificant, combined with the ordinary pressures of any job, they can have a major impact on a person's job satisfaction and performance.

Adding some international flair to any kind of career choice, however, can be an enriching experience—in more ways than one. Think about it. Are you ready to work your way around the world?

 TRY IT OUT

BUSINESS BRIEFING

Pick a country, any country. Go online and to the library to find out as much information as you can about the types of products they make and those they bring in from other places. A great source of information is the Cyber School Bus "Country at a Glance," at http://cyberschoolbus.un.org/infonation/index.asp. Either click on a favorite spot on the world map or scroll down to where it says "select a country" to find all kinds of useful information about the country of your choice. Another good spot to visit is the Peace Corps' Kids World Web site at http://www.peacecorps.gov/kids/world/africa/mali.html.

Pretend you need to brief the CEO of your company for a business trip and compile a background sheet on what you learn about the country's economy.

MIND YOUR MANNERS

When doing business in other parts of the world, it always pays to know what the local version of "Miss Manners" has to say about polite behavior. Polite in one place might be considered outrageous someplace else. It is never fun (or profitable) to be on the wrong side of a cultural faux pas.

Go online to the Executive Planet Web site at http://www.executiveplanet.com and pick a country that interests you. Read through the business culture guide and make a list of at least five do's and don'ts for conducting business politely in that country.

✔ CHECK IT OUT

🖱 ON THE WEB

CLICK AROUND THE WORLD

Do some online globe-trotting at Web sites such as:

- ♀ CNN Online News at http://www.cnn.com/EDUCATION
- ♀ National Geographic at http://www.nationalgeographic.com/kids
- ♀ Student News Net at http://www.studentnewsnet.com
- ♀ Time for Kids at http://www.timeforkids.com
- ♀ Wall Street Journal at http://www.wsjclassroom.com

SHOW ME THE MONEY AROUND THE WORLD

Find about more about the global economy at Web sites like:

- ♀ Before you take your business global, try running an online lemonade stand at http://www.coolmath-games.com/lemonade

- Climb aboard the United Nation's Cyber School Bus to find a world of information at http://www.un.org/Pubs/CyberSchoolBus
- Explore the world with the boomerang box at http://www.apl.com/boomerangbox
- Find out how much your allowance is worth in other countries at http://www.xe.com/ucc
- Track the gang of 15 as they spend money around the world at http://ecedweb.unomaha.edu/gang1.htm

AT THE LIBRARY

GOOD READS ON GLOBAL TRADE

Find out more about the world of international business in books such as:

Brown, Jeff M. *The Kids' Guide to Business.* Seattle: Teaching KidsBusiness.com, 2004.

Burgess, John. *World Trade.* New York: Chelsea House Publications, 2001.

Cooper, Adrian. *Fair Trade?: A Look at the Way the World is Today.* Corona, Calif.: Stargazer Books, 2005.

Cribb, Joe and Laura Buller. *Money.* New York: DK Children, 2005.

Frost, Randall, and Tina Schwartzenberger. *The Globalization of Trade.* Mankato, Minn.: Smart Apple Media, 2003.

Lewin, Ted. *How Much?: Visiting Markets Around the World.* New York: HarperCollins, 2006.

WITH THE EXPERTS

Academy of International Business
The Eli Broad College of Business
Michigan State University
Seven Eppley Center
East Lansing, MI 48824-1121
http://aib.msu.edu

International Chamber of Commerce
1212 Avenue of the Americas
New York, NY 10036-1689
http://www.iccwbo.org

U.S. Council for International Business
1212 Avenue of the Americas, Suite 1800
New York, NY 10036-1689
http://www.uscib.org

GET ACQUAINTED

Michael Harney,
International Businessperson

CAREER PATH

CHILDHOOD ASPIRATION:
Too busy being a kid to think about it much.

FIRST JOB: Dishwasher at a hotel.

CURRENT JOB: Vice president of Harney & Sons.

Michael Harney graduated from Cornell University with a degree in hotel management. He was lucky enough to land his first big job in Paris, where he worked in a wine-related tourism business. The job entailed a little of this and a little of that, and it eventually resulted in his working as a wine taster. Next on Harney's career map was a stop in the accounting department at a resort in the Virgin Islands. That was followed by eight years in Chicago where he ran a small boutique hotel that catered to an international clientele.

A FAMILY TRADITION
In the meantime, Harney's father had built a gourmet tea company back home in Connecticut and needed some help. With a business called Harney & Sons, Harney was the only man for the job (since his brother already worked there).

Now, Harney is a vital part of the thriving business. As the company Web site explains, Harney "travels the world searching for renowned varieties as well as exciting new infusions, from Germany to India," and recent trips were made to China and France—all in a quest to find the perfect teas! Another benefit of working in the family business is that he can take his kids along on his trips. One year he took his then 10-year-old son to Japan, where he loved the sushi. He also took his oldest son to China, Japan, and Taiwan, where he took lots of photos.

JUST A SPOT OF TEA

Tea taster is one of Harney's most important functions at the company. To do it right, he measures a dime's worth of tea into a cup of hot water and lets it brew for five minutes. Then he uses several senses to evaluate the results. First, he looks at the remains of the loose tea leaves. Then comes the most important step—smelling it. Taste is the last step. But, like wine tasters, tea tasters don't gulp down a sample; instead, they swish it around in their mouths and then spit it out.

How does Harney judge whether it's good tea or not? Experience helps, but the true sign of a good tea is one that makes your mouth move up into a smile.

A BIG WORLD OUT THERE

All things considered, Harney thinks it's a great time to be an American doing business around the world. Even though many of the people he trades with can speak English, Harney makes a point of learning at least a few phrases in the host country's language. It's a way to show respect for them. He also tries to understand where they are coming from by learning as much as he can about their country and culture.

To see photos from one of Harney's latest trips abroad, go to the company Web site at http://www.harney.com/travel.html.

International Relief Worker

SHORTCUTS

GO to the video store and rent the movie *Volunteers* for a humorous look at relief work.

READ *100 Jobs in Social Change* by Harley Jebens (New York: IDG Books, 1997).

TRY volunteering for a local relief organization.

SKILL SET

✔ TRAVEL
✔ ADVENTURE
✔ TALKING

WHAT IS AN INTERNATIONAL RELIEF WORKER?

For people in trouble, international relief workers are often the human equivalent of Superman. Among the first ones on the scene of the world's most dire situations, these people are quite often—and quite literally—lifesavers. The help extended by international relief workers takes many different forms, for instance:

- ☼ An international relief worker is a *doctor* who gives desperately needed medical care to children and families in underdeveloped and impoverished areas of the world.
- ☼ An international relief worker is a *Peace Corps volunteer* helping farmers grow healthy food for their communities.
- ☼ An international relief worker is a *carpenter* working with organizations such as Habitat for Humanity to build decent, affordable housing all around the world.
- ☼ An international relief worker is *part of a Red Cross team* that travels anywhere in the world on a moment's notice when disaster strikes. They bring food and clean water, and they assist with cleanup.

International Relief Worker

- ☀ An international relief worker is a *teacher* teaching English or any number of other subjects in schools found in both large cities and small villages around the world.
- ☀ An international relief worker *delivers shoe boxes* lovingly packed with toys, candy, and toiletries to children in war-torn areas who wouldn't have them otherwise.
- ☀ And, an international relief worker *provides aid* to victims of violent conflicts—sometimes at considerable risk to themselves.

These are just a handful of jobs that are performed by international relief workers; there are many more. Just as there are many different kinds of international relief jobs, there are many different international relief organizations, ranging from religious organizations to groups that protect human rights or the environment. All this diversity provides an amazing array of opportunities for people with all kinds of talents, education, and experience. Blending personal passions with a profession is what this kind of work is all about.

There are also many different career paths for an international relief worker, depending on what you want to do. Useful college degrees include education, engineering, agriculture, medicine, and social sciences. Some positions require master's degrees. Other positions call for skill in trades such as plumbing, electrical wiring, or carpentry.

In addition, almost any type of administrative or managerial position available in other types of organizations is also available in international relief agencies. These include program directors who manage various projects or departments, development directors who raise money to support relief efforts, and volunteer coordinators who organize the volunteers.

Speaking of volunteers, many international relief workers volunteer their services on a part-time basis. They have regular jobs most of the year and go on relief trips during their vacation time. For example, a lot of doctors with thriving practices in the United States volunteer a few weeks every year to offer medical services to needy people in every corner of the world. For those with families or those who can't afford to do relief work full time, these short-term trips are a great way to make the world a better place.

International relief work is not a route to monetary riches. For example, the Peace Corps pays living expenses for volunteers, and at the end of their assignments they receive approximately $6,000 to help workers transition to life back at home. Most assignments last two years. Any way you add the numbers, it's not a lot of money. However, the experience itself can be invaluable when it comes time to look for other types of work.

International relief workers often see parts of the world that most people never see. And they go to sleep at night knowing they have made a significant contribution to their world—a feeling that money can't buy.

☞ TRY IT OUT

HERE I COME TO SAVE THE DAY!
Visit AlertNet at http://www.alertnet.org. It has the latest news and up-to-date information on disaster and relief efforts around the world. Acquaint yourself with a crisis and identify

a group needing aid. Imagine you are in charge of a relief organization that wants to help.

You will have to answer a lot of questions: What kinds of volunteers are needed? Medical? Technical? Construction crews? Do they need food, building materials, medical supplies, or clothing? What other resources will you need to provide relief? How will you recruit the volunteers that you need?

Prepare a disaster relief plan outlining the needs and how you will meet them.

GO AHEAD, CHANGE THE WORLD

Talk is cheap. If you really want to make a difference, start now. If you begin looking now, chances are good that you can find a relief project to work on during your next summer vacation. An international trip may be as close as your local school or place of worship. Many churches offer teenagers an opportunity to participate in summer mission trips. Check it out! If that doesn't work out, there are some resources you can check online.

International World Changers (http://www.thetask.org/iwc .htm) sponsors youth trips every summer to places such as Kenya, Jordan, South Africa, and Sudan. Students participate in activities such as construction, English language camps, boys and girls clubs, sports outreach, and scripture distribution.

Habitat for Humanity International (http://www.habitat .org/GV/) offers international trips through their Global Village Program. Participants around the world work with locals to build decent and affordable housing.

Or go ahead and start your own Kids Care Club. Find out how at http:///www.kidscare.org.

CHARITY BEGINS AT HOME

Maybe an international trip is not in your immediate future. There are plenty of opportunities for you to get a taste for relief work right here. There are probably some right in your hometown. Check your phone book for local chapters of the American Red Cross, Habitat for Humanity, and the Salvation Army. Rescue missions and soup kitchens are always in need of volunteers. Your local Junior League can also point you in the direction of some local volunteer jobs. Even if, after volunteering, you decide that a career in relief work is not for you, the experience you gain will be valuable to you regardless of your career choice.

Spend some time online for more info on international relief work. Here are some sites to get you started:

- Find links to members of InterAction, the nation's largest coalition of relief, development, and refugee agencies, at http://www.interaction.org/members/index.html.
- Watch a short video online about children in Romania at the Children's Relief Network site at http://www.romanianchildren.org.
- Link to different relief organizations from Reliefnet at http://www.reliefnet.org.
- Search through a database of jobs in disaster relief at http://www.alertnet.org/thepeople/jobs/index.htm
- Take a virtual tour of a refugee camp and find out about the work that Doctors without Borders does at http://www.dwb.org.
- Join Amnesty International and their international human rights movement at http://www.amnestyusa.org.
- Samaritan's Purse is a nondenominational evangelical Christian organization that provides spiritual and physical aid to needy people around the world. See what they are up to at http://www.samaritanspurse.org.
- Learn everything you ever wanted to know about the Peace Corps at http://www.peacecorps.gov. Be sure to check out the special kids section.
- The American Red Cross site at http://www.redcross.org will give you some insight into the many different kinds of relief work that they do.
- CARE is one of the world's largest private international relief and development organizations: http://www.care.org.

✔ CHECK IT OUT

🖱 ON THE WEB
DASTARDLY DISASTERS

What do tsunamis, droughts, floods, earthquakes, and hurricanes have in common? They are all potentially dangerous natural disasters that often leave huge, awful messes behind. One of the most devastating disasters to hit the United States in recent years was Hurricane Katrina. This hurricane killed hundreds of people, destroyed thousands of homes, and pretty much wiped out several towns in Louisiana and Mississippi. Find out more about the lessons learned from this terrible tragedy at:

- 💡 http://www.pbs.org/wgbh/nova/orleans
- 💡 http://teacher.scholastic.com/scholasticnews/indepth/hurricanekatrina
- 💡 http://www.timeforkids.com/TFK/teachers/search/1,28225,,O.html?keyword=hurricane+katrina

You can also find information by using your favorite Internet search engine to run a search using the words *Hurricane Katrina*.

📚 AT THE LIBRARY
GOOD READS ON DOING GOOD

Check out some of the diverse opportunities for long- and short-term international relief work with some of these titles:

Barnard, Bryn. *Dangerous Planet: Natural Disasters that Changed History*. New York: Crown Books for Young Readers, 2003.

Bingham, Jane. *The Red Cross Movement*. Chicago, Ill.: Raintree, 2004.

Binns, Tristan Boyer. *FEMA: Federal Emergency Management Agency.* Chicago: Heinemann, 2003.

Church, Diane. *Protecting the Environment: Charities at Work.* Danbury, Conn.: Franklin Watts, 2004.

————. *Working With Children: Charities at Work.* Danbury, Conn.: Franklin Watts, 2004.

————. *Working With People with Disabilities: Charities at Work.* Danbury, Conn.: Franklin Watts, 2004.

Kjelle, Marylou Morano. *Helping Hands: America Responds to the Events of September 11, 2001.* New York: Chelsea House Publications, 2002.

Morris, Ann, and Heidi Larson. *Tsunami: Helping Each Other.* Minneapolis: Lerner Publications, 2005.

 ## WITH THE EXPERTS

American Council for Voluntary International Action
1400 16th Street NW, Suite 210
Washington, DC 20036-2217
http://www.interaction.org

American Red Cross
2025 E Street NW
Washington, DC 20006-5009
http://www.redcross.org

American Society of Association Executives
The ASAE Building
1575 I Street NW
Washington, DC 20005-1103
http://www.asaenet.org

Independent Charities of America
21 Tamal Vista Boulevard, Suite 209
Corte Madera, CA 94925-1147
http://www.independentcharities.org

Society for Nonprofit Organizations
5820 Canton Center Road, Suite 165
Canton, MI 48187-2683
http://www.snpo.org

GET ACQUAINTED

Douglas Allen,
International Relief Worker

CAREER PATH

CHILDHOOD ASPIRATION:
To be a pilot.

FIRST JOB: Moving pallets
around with a forklift in a ware-
house in Peru.

CURRENT JOB: International
disaster relief unit director with
the American Red Cross.

AN INTERNATIONAL LIFE

Douglas Allen was born and spent his early years in South
America, where his father worked as a mining engineer. It
was an interesting start to a life that got even more interesting when Allen was about 10 or 11; that's when he outgrew
the education provided where his family was living, and he
was sent away to boarding school—first in Scotland and then
in Massachusetts. He remembers that being 5,000 or 6,000
miles away from home was not a particularly fun experience, but he admits that he did get a great education in the
process.

Allen's first encounter with an international relief agency
was when he was nine, spending the summer in Canada—he
earned a lifesaving swimming badge from the Red Cross.
Later, while attending college in Florida, Allen got involved
helping to teach English to the children of migrant workers.

From the very beginning, Allen's career had an international flavor. His first job out of college was working the Latin
American desk at a Canadian bank, where he was responsible
for merchant lending, and it required a lot of traveling. After

that, he and some friends from business school started an import/export consulting business—more travel.

CAREER TO GO

Next up was a stint as director of development and public affairs for the Alexandria, Virginia, chapter of the American Red Cross. Hurricane Andrew hit while Allen was on the job, sending Allen and 14,000 volunteers to the rescue. Allen said that while a typical disaster requires about three weeks of help, this hurricane was so devastating that the project lasted more than a year.

After a couple of years with the Alexandria chapter, Allen moved on to the D.C. chapter. In 1991, he took his current job at the Red Cross national headquarters. Now he's in charge of a staff of 10, who work to prepare for, cope with, and manage all kinds of disaster relief efforts.

Since he's been on the job, he's been summoned to the scene of embassy bombings, tsunamis, earthquakes, hurricanes, floods, and mudslides. His work has taken him to virtually every corner of the world, including New Guinea, Colombia, Lebanon, Turkey, India, and Venezuela.

He says that regardless of the circumstances, the Red Cross starts each effort by conducting a needs assessment, a system that helps them figure out how to meet the basic needs of the most vulnerable people. Often that translates into targeting senior citizens and young children first and providing the most basic of resources—shelter, clean water, medicine, and food.

Allen says that sometimes the greatest challenge is not in having enough supplies but in finding ways to distribute them. That process can get tricky especially when trying to coordinate efforts with all kinds of other volunteers and organizations.

FACING TRAGEDY

No matter how you look at it, this is tough work. Yes, it is rewarding beyond words, but being confronted with so much tragedy is hard for anyone to deal with. Allen says that it helps to "keep the face of the beneficiaries right in front of you and you won't make many mistakes." He says one look at the grateful face of someone you are helping is all that it takes to put everything in perspective.

HELP FOR THE HELPERS

Allen cautions that this is not a job for people who simply want to travel and help people. His jet-setting lifestyle may sound glamorous to outsiders, but it's hard work, plain and simple. Relief work is an industry—with its own standards, vocabulary, and procedures, just like any other industry. It's not enough to see a need and try to fix it. In fact, some relief efforts are actually hampered by well-meaning volunteers who come to a place with unrealistic expectations.

Future relief workers would do well to start from the ground up, according to Allen. Volunteer with local nonprofit organizations. Take disaster training classes offered by Red Cross chapters all over the country. Get involved with a Red Cross disaster relief team. It will give you a better idea of what to expect and prepare you to provide help that really helps.

Military Serviceperson

SHORTCUTS

GO visit your local military recruiter.

READ about the history of some of America's greatest battles from the Revolutionary War to the Iraq War.

TRY running farther or faster than you have ever run before.

WHAT IS A MILITARY SERVICEPERSON?

Preserve, protect, and defend—that's what military service-people are charged to do each day. In the United States, there are four basic military branches, each with a different and vital role to play. The army serves on land with ground troops and tanks, the navy serves in ships that roam the world's oceans, the air force serves in planes and jets in the air, and the marines help with support forces on land, in the air, and at sea. Two supplementary services also lend a hand to keep our country safe—the Coast Guard protects our coastal waterways, and the National Guard provides military support in times of crisis.

You may be amazed to discover how many choices you'll have if you opt for a career in the military. Together, the services offer more than 4,000 different military jobs—with both full- and part-time opportunities available. Some people make a career out of military service and devote 20 or 30 years of their lives to it. Others join the military to train for a career they want to pursue outside the military. It's a great way to gain excellent skills and work experience, develop your leadership ability, and earn benefits toward a college education.

Military Serviceperson

Military jobs include front-line combat positions as well as electronic-related jobs in communications and intelligence, health care, administrative support, skilled trades such as carpenters and plumbers, and positions in service and supply. There are also highly technical positions in meteorology, surveying, and mapping as well as more creative ones in photography and music.

Military personnel are divided into two separate categories: officers and enlisted personnel. Officers are the military's leaders. They start out as first lieutenants, with the cream of the crop ultimately earning the status of general. Personnel in either category gain rank and increased responsibilities and pay through exemplary performance and time in service.

Currently about 224,000 commissioned officers serve in the military. Officers must have a college degree. Many receive their degrees and military training from a military academy such as West Point, the Naval Academy, or the Air Force Academy. Competition to enter one of the academies can be keen. To enter, you need to meet all the basic requirements, plus be no more than 23 years old, be unmarried with no dependents, have excellent grades and test scores, and be nominated by a member of the U.S. Congress. The Coast Guard Academy does not require congressional nomination, but accepts students on a competitive basis.

Joining the Reserve Officers' Training Corps (ROTC) is another way to become a military officer.

This program works with students at certain colleges around the country, providing military training during the school semesters and requiring full summers of military service. ROTC students receive college scholarships in exchange for serving on active duty for a certain number of years after they graduate from college.

In addition to officers, there are about 162,000 enlisted people recruited into the military each year. To enlist in any branch of the service, you must have a high school diploma or its equivalent and meet vision, height, weight, and overall health minimums. In addition, you must be over the age of 17, be a U.S. citizen or permanent resident, and pass a written test.

Whether officer or enlisted, everyone goes through six to 11 weeks of basic training (boot camp) plus additional training in their specialty area. Depending upon which occupation you choose, you could spend more than a year in initial training. Often the training is rigorous, and seemingly impossible at first. Some of it is designed to test your mental and physical limits, and it can be a real growing-up experience.

All military branches are open to both men and women. Only a few front-line combat jobs are limited to men; otherwise the opportunity, requirements, and standards are equal for all.

Serving in the military is different from working in a civilian job. It's not just a job; it's a lifestyle. Most bases and ships are like cities unto themselves. Whether for a few years or for a lifetime, it can be a great way to see the world and serve your country.

☞ TRY IT OUT

THE HISTORY OF WAR

Get a better sense of how war has shaped America's history by reading various titles in the *America at War* series published by Facts On File. Each title uses pictures and words to explain the why, when, what, who, and where questions associated with major military conflicts involving the United States. Separate titles in the series focus on the Revolutionary War, the War of 1812, the U.S. Mexican War, the Civil War, the Spanish-American War, World War I, World War II, the Korean War, the Vietnam War, the Persian Gulf War, and the Iraq War.

Use the information you find in books like these, and by searching the Internet using a favorite search engine such as http://www.yahoo.com or http://www.google.com, to create a timeline showing when each war began and ended.

BOOT CAMP

Do you have what it takes to make it through boot camp? You might be surprised. One way to find out is to get together with a few friends and stage your own boot camp. Plan several challenging activities such as a physical fitness test, an obstacle course at a local playground, and maybe even a map-reading activity. Be careful, but push yourselves a bit to find out how tough you really are.

Or, next time your school offers the Presidential Physical Fitness Test, get yourself into shape to pass every event. Practice, practice, practice—that's what it always takes to succeed.

JUNIOR ROTC

Many high schools offer junior ROTC programs that provide military training for teens. Find out if your high school has a program and plan to join. It's a great way to find out if the military life is a good choice for you—and to find out how you look in a uniform!

✔ CHECK IT OUT

🖰 ON THE WEB
VIRTUAL MILITARY

Each of the military branches has its own Web site. Check them out at:

- ☼ Air Force at http://www.airforce.com
- ☼ Army at http://www.goarmy.com

☼ Coast Guard at http://gocoastguard.com
☼ Marines at http://www.marines.com
☼ Navy at http://www.navy.com

You'll also find out more about the many career opportunities in all branches of the military at these Web sites:

☼ http://www.todaysmilitary.com
☼ http://www.myfuture.com
☼ http://www.militarycareers.com

 AT THE LIBRARY

READ ALL ABOUT IT

Before you sign up for military service, make sure you have all the facts. It's not a decision to be made on a whim. Once you sign, you're in and there is no getting out until your time is up. For more information about opportunities available in the military, look through books such as these:

Bell-Rehwoldt, Sheri. *Military*. Farmington Hills, Mich.: Lucent Books, 2005.

Benson, Michael. *The U.S. Marine Corps*. Minneapolis: Lerner, 2004.

Bryan, Nichol. *The National Guard*. Minneapolis: Checkerboard Books, 2002.

Green, Michael, and Gladys Green. *The U.S. Rangers at War*. Mankato, Minn.: Capstone, 2003.

Libal, Joyce. *Military and Elite Forces Officer*. Broomhall, Pa.: Mason Crest, 2003.

Nordman, Cindey. *The U.S. Army and Military Careers*. Berkeley Heights, N.J.: Enslow, 2006.

Parks, Peggy J. *Fighter Pilot*. Farmington Hills, Mich.: Kid Haven Press, 2005.

Roberts, Jeremy. *U.S. Army Special Operations Forces*. Minneapolis: Lerner, 2004.

🗣️ WITH THE EXPERTS

United States Air Force Academy
Colorado Springs, CO 80840-5025
http://www.usafa.af.mil

United States Coast Guard Academy
31 Mohegan Avenue
New London, CT 06320-8103
http://www.cga.edu

United States Military Academy
West Point, NY 10996
http://www.usma.army.mil

United States Naval Academy
121 Blake Road
Annapolis, MD 21402-1300
http://www.usna.edu

GET ACQUAINTED

Todd Arnold
Military Serviceperson

CAREER PATH

CHILDHOOD ASPIRATION:
To be a professional baseball player.

FIRST JOB: Mowing the lawn in his city park.

CURRENT JOB: Brigade Data Officer, 22nd Signal Brigade, U.S. Army.

A FAMILY AFFAIR

Ever since Captain Todd Arnold was a little boy, he wanted to go to West Point, the army's prestigious military academy. Two of his uncles went there and it always seemed like a big deal to his family. As he got older, he realized that it was a great school and that the military could provide him with many great opportunities. After going through a challenging application process, Arnold was accepted and left his home in North Dakota for the grueling "beast barracks" initiation program. Once he made it through that, he started a four-year college program that included challenging academics and military training. According to Arnold, attending a military college was a very trying experience. He found that everything is very structured and that students are not allowed to stray very far off of the school's predetermined path. But like most worthwhile things in life, the experience had both good points and bad. Arnold says that the best part for him was the challenging environment, while the worst part was that the environment and high expectations placed students under a lot of pressure.

COMPUTER WAR ZONE
After graduating from West Point and completing his military branch basic course, Arnold was assigned to his first military duty post in Germany. With the country at war, the better part of this overseas experience was spent in Iraq. Arnold was there when the first bombs fell and again a year or so later, but thanks to his highly prized technical skills, he was not in a combat position.

His job as the brigade's data network engineer was to set up and manage the technology used by military personnel serving in Iraq. Although the circumstances and specific types of technology are a bit different, this is the type of job one might find in a Fortune 500 company. In some ways, the work is similar to what a civilian might do. A typical day consists of taking in new requirements from the users and engineering the best solutions he can come up with. If he wasn't designing or redesigning a solution due to requirement changes, he was busy troubleshooting issues in the network.

Of course, a big difference is the danger. The size of the network itself was enormous and the pace was intense. Arnold

says that problems occur more frequently and the solution always needs to happen now. In many cases, keeping the lines of communication open could literally mean the difference between life and death for troops in combat zones. Although Arnold says he was lucky because his work was done in a safe and well-guarded location, things could get a little tense at times. To keep things normal, he says that he'd get together with friends to watch movies or TV episodes on DVD.

MOVING ON

After completing his tours of duty in Germany and Iraq, Arnold was relocated to a university in Pennsylvania, where he will pursue a master's degree. The degree will prepare him for what is known in the military as a secondary specialty. After that, Arnold hopes to spend the rest of his time in the military working as a network engineer.

Travel Agent

SKILL SET
- ✔ TRAVEL
- ✔ TALKING
- ✔ COMPUTERS

WHAT IS A TRAVEL AGENT?

You've just come back from a relaxing lunch, and your telephone rings. You are expecting a potential customer looking to book a fabulous vacation. Instead, it is an irate customer calling from Timbuktu. The hotel where you sent him has no record of a reservation ever being made, and there are no vacancies. Your customer is in a strange place with no place to stay and is furious with you! Can you keep your cool and find a way out of a horrible situation? Can you calm your customer down, take some responsibility for the problem (even though it may not be your fault), and restore his faith in you (because you want him to book trips with you again)? If not, don't read any further because this scenario and others like it are a regular part of a travel agent's job. A travel agent makes all kinds of travel arrangements for all kinds of clients.

A lot of detail work goes into planning the perfect vacation. Travel agents have to be familiar with all sorts of different destinations and travel packages. Some agents specialize in certain types of trips (such as cruises) or specific regions of the world (such as Europe). When a potential customer comes in, the travel agent has to listen to find out exactly what kind of trip the customer wants. Is it a honeymoon, a business trip, or a family vacation? What is the customer's budget? Can she afford first class all the way or does she need to pinch her pennies?

Some customers know exactly where they want to go, while others look to their travel agent for a lot of guidance in selecting just the right trip. The agent uses special computer programs as well as travel savvy to find the best options for the customer. This process often involves some give and take as the agent works with the client to work out all the kinks and get all the details straight.

Next comes actually booking the trip, which is, after all, the travel agent's goal in the whole process. This step is especially important since commissions from airlines, hotels, rental car agencies, and cruise lines is how travel agents get paid.

Once a trip has been purchased, the travel agent goes about the business of making it happen. This involves making airline and hotel reservations, booking rental cars and making arrangements for tours, sightseeing, and recreational activities. When international travel is involved, the travel agent may walk clients through the process of obtaining a passport and provide information about customs regulations and currency exchange rates. A good travel agent is also a good source of tips on where to eat and what to see in places all over the world.

One of the benefits of working as a travel agent is discounted travel. Also, agents sometimes get to take FAM (familiarization) trips at little cost to them. These trips allow them to familiarize themselves with different destinations. They check out hotels and attractions so they can better sell the destination to their customers.

It is possible to get an entry-level job, such as receptionist, at a travel agency and receive on-the-job training to become an agent. However, most agencies require some college or vocational training. Some specialized travel agent training programs take just 6 to 12 weeks to complete. Some schools also offer two- or four-year degrees in travel and tourism.

The Internet has changed how travel agents work in huge ways. It actually competes with them for customers because it makes it easy for people to find information, book arrangements, and plan trips from their computers. As a result, travel agents have had to get creative in the range of services they offer customers. Many have found success by specializing in luxury travel, group excursions, or handling the details associated with more complex travel agendas. They add value to their services by putting together unique trips to exotic or popular destinations and find ways to save their customers time and money.

 TRY IT OUT

YOU'RE HIRED!

Help! The local travel agency is swamped. They need some help getting through the peak travel season, and you're the person for the job. Here's the skinny on your first client: A family of four wants to take a trip to Honolulu, Hawaii, for two weeks in January. Use the following Web sites to find them the best airfares and hotel and car rental deals.

Airlines
- Delta at http://www.delta.com
- United Airlines at http://www.united.com
- American Airlines at http://www.aa.com

Hotels
- Hilton Hotels at http://www.hilton.com
- Hyatt Hotels and Resorts http://www.hyatt.com
- Marriott Hotels at http://www.marriott.com

Car Rental
- ☼ Alamo at http://www.alamo.com
- ☼ Avis at http://www.avis.com
- ☼ Budget at http://www.budget.com

Or, make the most of online travel resources at some of these one-stop travel planning Web sites:

- ☼ Expedia at http://www.expedia.com
- ☼ Hotwire at http://www.hotwire.com
- ☼ Orbitz at http://www.orbitz.com
- ☼ Travelocity at http://www.travelocity.com

Play around with the arrival and departure dates and see if that affects the price. Then prepare a summary for a budget trip, mid-priced trip, and luxury trip including places to go and things to see.

PICK A LOCATION, ANY LOCATION

Select a travel destination that seems exciting to you and research it thoroughly. Start at http://www.lonelyplanet.com/worldguide or http://www.geographica.com. Find out everything you can about the location including how you get there, what hotels are there, what makes it special, what the currency exchange rate is, and seasonal weather conditions. Use the information you gather to make a travel brochure that sells that destination.

✔ CHECK IT OUT

🖱 ON THE WEB

CYBER DESTINATIONS

There are some great travel sites on the Web. Take a look at these to get started:

- ☼ Check out Travel Zoo's guide to travel sales and specials at http://www.travelzoo.com.
- ☼ The Intrepid Traveler at http://www.intrepidtraveler .com is an informative and educational site for those people who want to see the world.

☼ Visit http://www.traveltrade.com, the business paper of the travel industry. It has news of interest to travel agents.

☼ Venture out into the world's rain forests at http://www .rainforestweb.org/Rainforest_Information/Sites_for_Kids.

☼ Explore some of the world's most adventurous destinations at http://www.nationalgeographic.com/ adventure.

☼ Climb aboard and take a virtual voyage around the world at http://www.beworldwise.org.

☼ Take a stroll down Kid Avenue at http://www.aaa .com/misc/mainpg.htm.

☼ Get ideas for your next family vacation at http:// www.travelforkids.com.

📚 AT THE LIBRARY

BOOK A TRIP TO THE LIBRARY

Visit the library and get the inside scoop on a career as a travel agent. Start with a handful of these books:

Burgan, Michael. *Travel Agent: Career Exploration.* Mankato, Minn.: Capstone, 2000.

Colbert, Judy. *Career Opportunities in the Travel Industry.* New York: Ferguson, 2004.

Milne, Robert. *Opportunities in Travel Careers.* New York: McGraw Hill, 2003.

Plawin, Paul. *Careers for Travel Buffs and Other Restless Types.* New York: McGraw Hill, 2003.

A WORLD WIDE READ

See the world from the comfort of your own room with this delightful series of books:

Green, Jen. *Destination Detective: Japan.* Chicago: Raintree, 2006.

———. *Destination Detective: Mexico.* Chicago: Raintree, 2006.

Mason Paul. *Destination Detective: France*. Chicago: Raintree, 2006.

———. *Destination Detective: Italy*. Chicago: Raintree, 2006.

———. *Destination Detective: Spain*. Chicago: Raintree, 2006.

Roy, Anita. *Destination Detective: India*. Chicago: Raintree, 2006

🗣 WITH THE EXPERTS

American Society of Travel Agents
1101 King Street, Suite 200
Alexandria, VA 22314-2963
http://www.astanet.com

Travel Industry Association of America
1100 New York Avenue NW, Suite 450
Washington, DC 20005-3934
http://www.tia.org

The Travel Institute
148 Linden Street, Suite 305
Wellesley, MA 02482-7916
http://www.thetravelinstitute.com

GET ACQUAINTED

Michele Abrate,
Travel Agent

CAREER PATH

CHILDHOOD ASPIRATION: To be an attorney.

FIRST JOB: Working in a dress shop.

CURRENT JOB: President of Armstrong & Hedges, purveyors of fine travel.

WHEN A VACATION IS NOT A VACATION

Michele Abrate had a hero when she was younger: it was Gladys Towles Root, a prominent trial lawyer in Los Angeles. She wanted to grow up to be just like her. But that was before an extended trip to Europe sparked her love of art and travel.

She majored in art history, graduated, and worked briefly for an art gallery, but she soon found herself right smack in the middle of an economic recession when cushy art jobs were few and far between. Abrate admits she's among those people who tend to give more thought to making their Christmas card list than to their career path, so she didn't have any overwhelming ambitions in the art world. She did, however, find it necessary to do something to pay the bills, so she took a job with a travel company specializing in carriage trade, which means most of the customers were wealthy.

There, she enjoyed the best sides of travel and honed her skills in sales and building relationships. The travel was plentiful and luxurious, and the people were interesting. By the time Abrate left that agency to manage another one, the travel bug had bitten and she was hooked.

ADVENTURES IN TRAVEL

With more than 25 years' experience in the travel industry, Abrate's career continues to blossom in exciting ways. When it comes to travel agencies, she's done it all—managed them, set up shop as an independent agent, worked as a temp in 60 different offices in just a three-year time span, and directed marketing activities for an upscale leisure travel business. She was even elected president of a professional association for travel agents, which gave her an opportunity to travel all over the world speaking about her profession.

All this experience helped Abrate eventually earn the distinction of certified travel consultant and instructor. This rigorous training credential is roughly the equivalent of earning a master's degree. Not a bad achievement for someone who never attended travel school!

One thing that Abrate has noticed over the years is that smaller agencies with a reputation for doing a certain kind

of travel seemed to enjoy a higher degree of success than those that do a little bit of everything. She also discovered an area of travel that wasn't getting much attention from other agencies—that of providing special travel opportunities just for women.

A TRIP OF A LIFETIME

Abrate is now president of a company that specializes in arranging once-in-a-lifetime trips for women. Whether it's a daffodil festival in Nantucket, a fully guided mother/daughter tour of Paris and Provence, or a cottage garden tour in England, Abrate's trips pull out all the stops. Through great contacts and lots of research, Abrate finds those out-of-the-way places and provides the extra touches that make each trip a memory to cherish.

Abrate says staging events like these takes more organization skills than you could imagine. It's a good thing that she is an astute multitasker who can juggle lots of projects at once. She says it's not unusual to be making some sort of contact with all seven continents in one day!

THINGS YOU DON'T LEARN IN TRAVEL SCHOOL

Succeeding in this business requires more than a love of travel, according to Abrate. There's a lot to learn and dues to pay along the way. She also says that you don't learn some of the most important lessons in travel school. For instance, she sees three skills as critical to success: sales savvy, marketing muscle, and negotiating know-how. Top that off with an ability to present yourself in a professional manner, and you've got that extra edge to write your own ticket as a travel agent.

BY THE WAY

You are invited to visit Abrate's Web site at http://www.teagardentravel.com to learn more about her business for yourself.

MAKE A DETOUR THAT TAKES YOU PLACES!

Let your imagination—and your most adventure-filled ambitions—take flight! There are endless ways to combine your skills, your interests, and your quest for adventure with a career that's just right for you. You may find the perfect career opportunity waiting for you around the corner or around the world! Go through the following lists and see what strikes your fancy. Once you find an intriguing idea or two, use the suggestions on pages 161–70 to find out more about it.

CAREERS THAT GET AROUND

ON LAND

automobile engineer
automotive engineer
army special forces officer
bus driver
dispatcher
heavy machinery operator

logistics manager
marine serviceperson
police officer
taxi driver
subway operator

AT SEA

The next list is a long one because it includes a surprising array of jobs on major cruise lines. Those big ships are like small cities on water, so just about anything you can do on dry land, you can also do at sea.

accountant
aerobics instructor
baker
bartender
bookkeeper
butcher
cabin steward
carpenter
cashier
casino dealer
chef
child-care provider
Coast Guard serviceperson
dancer
dance teacher
deckhand
dishwasher
disk jockey
diving instructor

doctor
entertainer
ferry operator
hairstylist
laundry worker
librarian
lifeguard
maintenance engineer
masseuse
merchant marine
navy SEAL
navy serviceperson
plumber
sailor
security officer
sports pro (especially in tennis
  and golf)
steward

IN THE AIR

With today's breed of supersonic jets, the world is more accessible than ever. Here are some ways to take flight with your career:

aerospace engineer
aircraft mechanic
air force serviceperson
airline ticket agent
air traffic controller
astronaut

baggage handler
flight attendant
helicopter weather reporter
meteorologist
pilot

MORE ADVENTUROUS CAREER CHOICES

THE SCIENCE OF ADVENTURE

Adventure lovers everywhere make sure to consider a career in science. It's hard to find another field that offers so many opportunities for discovery and challenge.

aerospace engineer
anthropologist
archaeologist
astronomer
biologist
botanist
ecologist
environmentalist
epidemiologist
geographer
geologist
marine biologist
nuclear physicist
petroleum engineer

ANIMAL ADVENTURES

If you've ever tried to train a puppy, you know that having anything to do with animals can be a real adventure.

animal ecologist
animal scientist
circus performer
exotic animal trainer
farmer

horse trainer
lion tamer
veterinarian
zookeeper

AROUND-THE-WORLD ADVENTURES

Here are some ways to work your way around the world:

air traffic controller
cruise director
deep sea fisherman
diplomat
flight attendant
helicopter pilot
merchant marine

race car driver
sailor
sea captain
tour guide
travel agent
truck driver

OUT-OF-THIS-WORLD ADVENTURE

You're sure to find plenty of adventure to go around in any of these space-related career ideas:

aerospace engineer
mission control specialist
satellite designer
satellite operator

spacecraft simulation engineer
space launch specialist
spacesuit designer

HELPFUL ADVENTURES

Doing good can be a good way to earn your keep.

bomb squad officer
fire marshal
personal trainer
police officer
politician

psychiatrist
psychologist
sports physician
storm chaser

DON'T STOP NOW!

GO FOR IT!

It's been a fast-paced trip so far. Take a break, regroup, and look at all the progress you've made.

1st Stop: Discover
You discovered some personal interests and natural abilities that you can start building a career around.

2nd Stop: Explore
You've explored an exciting array of career opportunities in these fields. You're now aware that your career can involve either a specialized area with many educational require-ments or that it can involve a practical application of skills with a minimum of training and experience.

At this point, you've found a couple careers that make you wonder, "Is this a good option for me?" Now it's time to put it all together and make an informed, intelligent choice. It's time to get a sense of what it might be like to have a job like the one(s) you're considering. In other words, it's time to move on to step three and do a little experiment-ing with success.

3rd Stop: Experiment

By the time you finish this section, you'll have reached one of three points in the career planning process.

1. **Green light!** You found it. No need to look any further. This is the career for you. (This may happen to a lucky few. Don't worry if it hasn't happened yet for you. This whole process is about exploring options, experimenting with ideas, and, eventually, making the best choice for you.)

2. **Yellow light!** Close but not quite. You seem to be on the right path, but you haven't nailed things down for sure. (This is where many people your age end up, and it's a good place to be. You've learned what it takes to really check things out. Hang in there. Your time will come.)

3. **Red light!** Whoa! No doubt about it, this career just isn't for you. (Congratulations! Aren't you glad you found out now and not after you'd spent four years in college preparing for this career? Your next stop: Make a U-turn and start this process over with another career.)

Here's a sneak peek at what you'll be doing in the next section.

☀ First, you'll pick a favorite career idea (or two or three).

☀ Second, you'll link up with a whole world of great information about that career on the Internet (it's easier than you think).

☀ Third, you'll snoop around the library to find answers to the top 10 things you've just got to know about your future career.

☀ Fourth, you'll either write a letter or use the Internet to request information from a professional organization associated with this career.

☀ Fifth, you'll chat on the phone to conduct a telephone interview.

After all that you'll (finally!) be ready to put it all together in your very own Career Ideas for Kids career profile (see page 172).

Hang on to your hats and get ready to make tracks!

#1 NARROW DOWN YOUR CHOICES

You've been introduced to quite a few math- and money-related career ideas. You may also have some ideas of your own to add. Which ones appeal to you the most?

Write your top three choices in the spaces below. (Sorry if this is starting to sound like a broken record, but . . . if this book does not belong to you, write your responses on a separate sheet of paper.)

1. _____

2. _____

3. _____

#2 SURF THE NET

With the Internet, you have a world of information at your fingertips. The Internet has something for everyone, and it's getting easier to access all the time. An increasing number of libraries and schools are offering access to the Internet on their computers, or you may have a computer at home.

A typical career search will land everything from the latest news on developments in the field and course notes from universities to museum exhibits, interactive games, educational activities, and more. You just can't beat the timeliness or the variety of information available on the Web.

One of the easiest ways to track down this information is to use an Internet search engine, such as Yahoo! Simply type the topic you are looking for, and in a matter of seconds you'll have a list of options from around the world. For instance, if you are looking for information about companies that make candy, use the words "candy manufacturer" to start your search. It's fun to browse—you never know what you'll come up with.

Before you link up, keep in mind that many of these sites are geared toward professionals who are already working in a particular field. Some of the sites can get pretty technical. Just use the experience as a chance to nose around the field, hang out with the people who are tops in the field, and think about whether or not you'd like to be involved in a profession like that.

Specific sites to look for are the following:

Professional associations. Find out about what's happening in the field, conferences, journals, and other helpful tidbits.

Schools that specialize in this area. Many include research tools, introductory courses, and all kinds of interesting information.

Government agencies. Quite a few are going high-tech with lots of helpful resources.

Web sites hosted by experts in the field (this seems to be a popular hobby among many professionals). These Web sites are often as entertaining as they are informative.

If you're not sure where to go, just start clicking around. Sites often link to other sites. You may want to jot down notes about favorite sites. Sometimes you can even print information that isn't copyright protected; try the print option and see what happens.

Be prepared: Surfing the Internet can be an addicting habit! There is so much awesome information. It's a fun way to focus on your future.

Write the addresses of the three best Web sites that you find during your search in the space below (or on a separate sheet of paper if this book does not belong to you).

1. _____

2. _____

3. _____

#3 SNOOP AT THE LIBRARY

Take your list of favorite career ideas, a notebook, and a helpful adult with you to the library. When you get there, go to the reference section and ask the librarian to help you find books about careers. Most libraries will have at least one set

of career encyclopedias. Some of the larger libraries may also have career information on CD-ROM.

Gather all the information you can and use it to answer the following questions in your notebook about each of the careers on your list. Make sure to ask for help if you get stuck.

TOP 10 THINGS YOU NEED TO KNOW ABOUT YOUR CAREER

1. What is the purpose of this job?

   _____

2. What kind of place is this type of work usually done in? For example, would I work mostly in a busy office, outdoors, or in a laboratory?

   _____

3. What kind of time is required to do this job? For instance, is the job usually performed during regular daytime business hours or do people work various shifts around the clock?

   _____

4. What kinds of tools are used to do this job?

   _____

5. In what ways does this job involve working with other people?

   _____

6. What kind of preparation does a person need to qualify for this job?

   _____

7. What kinds of skills and abilities are needed to be successful in this type of work?

   _____

8. What's a typical day on the job like?

   _____

   _____

9. How much money can I expect to earn as a beginner?

   _____

10. What kind of classes do I need to take in high school to get ready for this type of work?

    _____

#4 GET IN TOUCH WITH THE EXPERTS

One of the best places to find information about a particular career is a professional organization devoted especially to that career. After all, these organizations are full of the best and the brightest professionals working in that particular field. Who could possibly know more about how the work gets done? There are more than 450,000 organizations in the United States, so there is bound to be an association related to just about any career you can possibly imagine.

There are a couple ways you can find these organizations:

1. Look at the "Check It Out—With the Experts" list following a career you found especially interesting in the Take A Trip! section of this book.

2. Go online and use your favorite search engine (such as http://www.google.com or http://yahoo.com) to find professional associations related to a career you are

interested in. You might use the name of the career, plus the words "professional association" to start your search. You're likely to find lots of useful information online, so keep looking until you hit pay dirt.

3. Go to the reference section of your public library and ask the librarian to help you find a specific type of association in a reference book called *Encyclopedia of Associations* (Farmington Hills, Mich.: Thomson Gale). Or, if your library has access to it, the librarian may suggest using an online database called *Associations Unlimited* (Farmington Hills, Mich.: Thomson Gale).

Once you've tracked down a likely source of information, there are two ways to get in touch with a professional organization.

1. Send an e-mail.

   Most organizations include a "contact us" button on their Web sites. Sometimes this e-mail is directed to a webmaster or a customer service representative. An e-mail request might look something like this:

   Subject: Request for Information
   Date: 2/1/2008 3:18:41 PM Eastern Standard Time
   From: janedoe@mycomputer.com
   To: webmaster@candyloversassociation.org

   I am a fifth-grade student, and I am interested in learning more about careers for candy lovers. Would you please send me any information you have about what people do in your industry?

   Thank you very much.
   Jane Doe

2. Write a letter requesting information.

   Your letter should be either typed on a computer or written in your best handwriting. It should include the date, the complete address of the organization you are contacting, a salutation or greeting, a brief

description of your request, and a signature. Make sure to include an address where the organization can reach you with a reply. Something like the following letter would work just fine.

Dear Sir or Madam:

I am a fifth-grade student, and I would like to learn more about what it is like to work in the candy lover profession. Would you please send me information about careers? My address is 456 Main Street, Anytown, USA 54321.

Thank you very much.

Sincerely,
Jane Doe

Write the names and addresses of the professional organizations you discover on a separate sheet of paper.

#5 CHAT ON THE PHONE

Talking to a seasoned professional—someone who experiences the job day in and day out—can be a great way to get the inside story on what a career is all about. Fortunately for you, the experts in any career field can be as close as the nearest telephone.

Sure, it can be a bit scary calling up an adult whom you don't know. But two things are in your favor:

1. They can't see you. The worst thing they can do is hang up on you, so just relax and enjoy the conversation.

2. They'll probably be happy to talk to you about their job. In fact, most people will be flattered that you've called. If you happen to contact someone who seems reluctant to talk, thank them for their time and try someone else.

Here are a few pointers to help make your telephone interview a success:

☼ Mind your manners and speak clearly.
☼ Be respectful of their time and position.
☼ Be prepared with good questions and
   take notes as you talk.

One more common sense reminder: be careful about giving out your address and DO NOT arrange to meet anyone you don't know without your parents' supervision.

TRACKING DOWN CAREER EXPERTS

You might be wondering by now how to find someone to interview. Have no fear! It's easy if you're persistent. All you have to do is ask. Ask the right people and you'll have a great lead in no time.

A few of the people to ask and sources to turn to are:

Your parents. They may know someone (or know someone who knows someone) who has just the kind of job you're looking for.

Your friends and neighbors. You might be surprised to find out how many interesting jobs these people have when you start asking them what they (or their parents) do for a living.

Librarians. Since you've already figured out what kinds of companies employ people in your field of interest, the next step is to ask for information about local employers. Although it's a bit cumbersome to use, a big volume called *Contacts Influential* can provide this kind of information.

Professional associations. Call, e-mail, or write to the professional associations you discovered using the activity on page 165 and ask for recommendations.

Chambers of commerce. The local chamber of commerce probably has a directory of employers, their specialties, and their phone numbers. Call the chamber, explain what you are looking for, and give them a chance to help their future workforce.

Newspaper and magazine articles. Find an article about the subject you are interested in. Chances are pretty good that it will mention the name of at least one expert in the field. The article probably won't include the person's phone number (that would be too easy), so you'll have to look for clues. Common clues include the name of the company that they work for, the town that they live in, and if the person is an author, the name of their publisher. Make a few phone calls and track them down (if long distance calls are involved, make sure to get your parents' permission first).

INQUIRING KIDS WANT TO KNOW

Before you make the call, make a list of questions to ask. You'll cover more ground if you focus on using the five W's (and the H) that you've probably heard about in your creative writing classes: Who? What? Where? When? How? and Why? For example:

1. Whom do you work for?

   _____

2. What is a typical workday like for you?

   _____

3. Where can I get some on-the-job experience?

   _____

4. When did you become a _____?
   (profession)

5. How much can you earn in this profession? (But remember, it's not polite to ask someone how much *he* or *she* earns.)

   _____

6. Why did you choose this profession?

   _____

Use a grid like the one below to keep track of the questions you ask in the boxes labeled "Q" and the answers you receive in the boxes labeled "A."

Who?	What?	Where?	When?	How?	Why?
Q	Q	Q	Q	Q	Q
A	A	A	A	A	A
Q	Q	Q	Q	Q	Q
A	A	A	A	A	A

One last suggestion: Add a professional (and very classy) touch to the interview process by following up with a thank-you note to the person who took time out of a busy schedule to talk with you.

#6 INFORMATION IS POWER

As you may have noticed, a similar pattern of information was used for each of the careers profiled in this book. Each entry included:

- ☀ a general description of the career
- ☀ Try It Out activities to give readers a chance to find out what it's really like to do each job
- ☀ a list of Web sites, library resources, and professional organizations to check for more information
- ☀ a get-acquainted interview with a professional

You may have also noticed that all the information you just gathered would fit rather nicely in a Career Ideas for Kids career profile of your own. Just fill in the blanks on the following pages to get your thoughts together (or, if this book does not belong to you, use a separate sheet of paper).

And by the way, this formula is one that you can use throughout your life to help you make fully informed career choices.

CAREER TITLE _____

WHAT IS A _____ ?

Use career encyclopedias and other resources to write a description of this career.

_____

_____

_____

_____

SKILL SET

✔ _____

✔ _____

✔ _____

☞ TRY IT OUT

Write project ideas here. Ask your parents and your teacher to come up with a plan.

_____

_____

_____

_____

_____

✔ CHECK IT OUT

🖱 ON THE WEB

List Internet addresses of interesting Web sites you find.

_____

_____

_____

_____

_____

📚 AT THE LIBRARY

List the titles and authors of books about this career.

_____

_____

_____

_____

_____

🗣 WITH THE EXPERTS

List professional organizations where you can learn more about this profession.

_____

_____

_____

_____

_____

GET ACQUAINTED

Interview a professional in the field and summarize your findings.

_____

_____

_____

_____

_____

_____

_____

_____

WHAT'S NEXT?

Whoa, everybody! At this point, you've put in some serious miles on your career exploration journey. Before you move on, let's put things in reverse for just a sec and take another look at some of the clues you uncovered about yourself when you completed the "Discover" activities in the Get in Gear chapter on pages 7 to 26.

The following activities will help lay the clues you learned about yourself alongside the clues you learned about a favorite career idea. The comparison will help you decide if that particular career idea is a good idea for you to pursue. It doesn't matter if a certain career sounds absolutely amazing. If it doesn't honor your skills, your interests, and your values, it's not going to work for you.

The first time you looked at these activities, they were numbered one through five as "Discover" activities. This time around they are numbered in the same order but labeled "Rediscover" activities. That's not done to confuse you (sure hope it doesn't!). Instead, it's done to drive home a very important point that this is an important process you'll want to revisit time and time again as you venture throughout your career—now and later.

First, pick the one career idea that you are most interested in at this point and write its name here (or if this book doesn't belong to you, blah, blah, blah—you know the drill by now):

_____

With that idea in mind, revisit your responses to the following Get in Gear activities and complete the following:

REDISCOVER #1:
WATCH FOR SIGNS ALONG THE WAY

Based on your responses to the statements on page 8, choose which of the following road signs best describes how you feel about your career idea:

- ☀ Green light—Go! Go! Go! This career idea is a perfect fit!
- ☀ Yellow light—Proceed with caution! This career idea is a good possibility, but you're not quite sure that it's the "one" just yet.
- ☀ Stop—Hit the brakes! There's no doubt about it—this career idea is definitely not for you!

REDISCOVER #2:
RULES OF THE ROAD

Take another look at the work-values chart you made on page 16. Now use the same symbols to create a work-values chart for the career idea you are considering. After you have all the symbols in place, compare the two charts and answer these questions:

- ☼ Does your career idea's **purpose** line up with yours? Would it allow you to work in the kind of **place** you most want to work in?
- ☼ What about the **time** commitment—is it in sync with what you're hoping for?
- ☼ Does it let you work with the **tools** and the kind of **people** you most want to work with?
- ☼ And, last but not least, are you willing to do what it takes to **prepare** for a career like this?

PURPOSE	PLACE	TIME
TOOLS	PEOPLE	PREPARATION

REDISCOVER #3: DANGEROUS DETOURS

Go back to page 16 and double-check your list of 10 careers that you hope to avoid at any cost.

Is this career on that list? ____Yes ____ No

Should it be? ____Yes ____ No

REDISCOVER #4:
ULTIMATE CAREER DESTINATION

Pull out the ultimate career destination brochure you made (as described on page 17). Use a pencil to cross through every reference to "my ideal career" and replace it with the name of the career idea you are now considering.

Is the brochure still true? _____ Yes _____ No

If not, what would you change on the brochure to make it true?

REDISCOVER #5:
GET SOME DIRECTION

Quick! Think fast! What is your personal Skill Set as discovered on page 26?

Write down your top three interest areas:

1. _____

2. _____

3. _____

What three interest areas are most closely associated with your career idea?

1. _____

2. _____

3. _____

Does this career's interest areas match any of yours?
_____ Yes _____ No

Now the big question: Are you headed in the right direction?

If so, here are some suggestions to keep you moving ahead:

- ☼ Keep learning all you can about this career—read, surf the Web, talk to people, and so on. In other words, keep using some of the strategies you used in the Don't Stop Now chapter on pages 159 to 174 to do all you can to make a fully informed career decision.
- ☼ Work hard in school and get good grades. What you do now counts! Your performance, your behavior, your attitude—all conspire to either propel you forward or hold you back.
- ☼ Get involved in clubs and other after-school activities to further develop your interests and skills. Whether it's student government, 4-H, or sports, these kinds of activities give you a chance to try new things and gain confidence in your abilities.

If not, here are some suggestions to help you regroup:

- ☼ Read other books in the Career Ideas for Kids series to explore options associated with your other interest areas.
- ☼ Take a variety of classes in school and get involved in different kinds of after-school activities to get a better sense of what you like and what you do well.
- ☼ Talk to your school guidance counselor about taking a career assessment test to help fine-tune your focus.
- ☼ Most of all, remember that time is on your side. Use the next few years to discover more about yourself, explore the options, and experiment with what it will take to make you succeed. Keep at it and look forward to a fantastic future!

HOORAY! YOU DID IT!

This has been quite a trip. If someone tries to tell you that this process is easy, don't believe them. Figuring out what you want to do with the rest of your life is heavy stuff, and it should be. If you don't put some thought (and some sweat and hard work) into the process, you'll get stuck with whatever comes your way.

You may not have things planned to a T. Actually, it's probably better if you don't. You'll change some of your ideas as you grow and experience new things. And, you may find an interesting detour or two along the way. That's OK.

The most important thing about beginning this process now is that you've started to dream. You've discovered that you have some unique talents and abilities to share. You've become aware of some of the ways you can use them to make a living—and perhaps make a difference in the world.

Whatever you do, don't lose sight of the hopes and dreams you've discovered. You've got your entire future ahead of you. Use it wisely.

PASSPORT TO YOUR FUTURE

Getting where you want to go requires patience, focus, and lots of hard work. It also hinges on making good choices. Following is a list of some surefire ways to give yourself the best shot at a bright future. Are you up to the challenge? Can you do it? Do you dare?

Put your initials next to each item that you absolutely promise to do.

___ ☼ Do my best in every class at school
___ ☼ Take advantage of every opportunity to get a wide variety of experiences through participation in sports, after-school activities, at my favorite place of worship, and in my community
___ ☼ Ask my parents, teachers, or other trusted adults for help when I need it
___ ☼ Stay away from drugs, alcohol, and other bad scenes that can rob me of a future before I even get there
___ ☼ Graduate from high school

SOME FUTURE DESTINATIONS

Wow! Look how far you've come! By now you should be well-equipped to discover, explore, and experiment your way to an absolutely fantastic future. To keep you headed in the right direction, this section will point you toward useful resources that provide more insight, information, and inspiration as you continue your quest to find the perfect career.

IT'S NOT JUST FOR NERDS

The school counselor's office is not just a place where teachers send troublemakers. One of its main purposes is to help students like you make the most of your educational opportunities. Most schools will have a number of useful resources, including career assessment tools (ask about the Self-Directed Search Career Explorer or the COPS Interest

Inventory—these are especially useful assessments for people your age). They may also have a stash of books, videos, and other helpful materials.

Make sure no one's looking and sneak into your school counseling office to get some expert advice!

AWESOME INTERNET CAREER RESOURCES

Your parents will be green with envy when they see all the career planning resources you have at your fingertips. Get ready to hear them whine, "But they didn't have all this stuff when I was a kid." Make the most of these cyberspace opportunities.

💡 **Adventures in Education**
http://adventuresineducation.org/middleschool
Here you'll find some useful tools to make the most of your education—starting now. Make sure to watch "The Great College Mystery," an online animation featuring Dr. Ed.

💡 **America's Career InfoNet**
http://www.acinet.org
Career sites don't get any bigger than this one! Compliments of the U.S. Department of Labor, and a chunk of your parent's tax dollars, you'll find all kinds of information about what people do, how much money they make, and where they work. Although it's mostly geared toward adults, you may want to take a look at some of the videos (the site has links to more than 450!) that show people at work.

💡 **ASVAB Career Exploration Program**
http://www.asvabprogram.com
This site may prove especially useful as you continue to think through various options. It includes sections

for students to learn about themselves, to explore careers, and to plan for their futures.

☼ Career Voyages
http://www.careervoyages.gov
This site will be especially helpful to you as you get a little older. It offers four paths to get you started: "Where do I start?" "Which industries are growing?" "How do I qualify and get a job?" and "Does education pay? How do I pay?" However, it also includes a special section especially for elementary school students. Just click the button that says "Still in elementary school?" or go to http://www.careervoyages.gov/students-elementary.cfm.

☼ Job Profiles
http://jobprofiles.org
This site presents the personal side of work with profiles of people working in jobs associated with agriculture and nature, arts and sports, business and communications, construction and manufacturing, education and science, government, health and social services, retail and wholesale, and other industries.

☼ Major and Careers Central
http://www.collegeboard.com/csearch/majors_careers
This site is hosted by the College Board (the organization responsible for a very important test called the SAT, which you're likely to encounter if you plan to go to college). It includes helpful information about how different kinds of subjects you can study in college can prepare you for specific types of jobs.

☼ Mapping Your Future
http://mapping-your-future.org/MHSS

This site provides strategies and resources for students as they progress through middle school and high school.

☼ My Cool Career
http://www.mycoolcareer.com
This site is where you can take free online self-assessment quizzes, explore your dreams, and listen to people with interesting jobs talk about their work.

☼ O*NET Online
http://online.onetcenter.org
This U.S. Department of Labor site provides comprehensive information about hundreds of important occupations. Although you may need to ask a parent or teacher to help you figure out how to use the system, it can be a good source of digging for nitty-gritty details about a specific type of job. For instance, each profile includes a description of the skills, abilities, and special knowledge needed to perform each job.

☼ Think College Early
http://www.ed.gov/students/prep/college
thinkcollege/early/edlite-tcehome.html
Even though you almost need a college degree just to type the Web address for this U.S. Department of Education site, it contains some really cool career information and helps you think about how college might fit into your future plans.

☼ What Interests You?
http://www.bls.gov/k12/
This Bureau of Labor Statistics site is geared toward students. It lets you explore careers by interests such as reading, building and fixing things, managing money, helping people, and more.

JOIN THE CLUB

Once you've completed eighth grade, you are eligible to check out local opportunities to participate in Learning for Life's career education programs. Some communities offer Explorer posts that sponsor activities with students interested in industries that include the arts and humanities, aviation, business, communications, engineering, fire service, health, law enforcement, law and government, science, skilled trades, or social services. To find a local office, go to http://www.learning-for-life.org/exploring/main.html and type your zip code.

Until then, you can go online and play *Life Choices*, a really fun and challenging game where you get one of five virtual jobs at http://www.learning-for-life.org/games/LCSH/index.html.

MORE CAREER BOOKS ESPECIALLY FOR KIDS

It's especially important that people your age find out all they can about as many different careers as they can. Books like the ones listed below can introduce all kinds of interesting ideas that you might not encounter in your everyday life.

Greenfeld, Barbara C., and Robert A. Weinstein. *The Kids' College Almanac: A First Look at College.* 3d ed. Indianapolis, Ind.: JIST Works, 2005.
Young Person's Occupational Outlook Handbook. Indianapolis, Ind.: JIST Works, 2005.

Following are brief descriptions of several series of books geared especially toward kids like you. To find copies of these books, ask your school or public librarian to help you search the library computer system using the name of the series.

Career Connections (published by UXL)

This extensive series features information and illustrations about jobs of interest to people interested in art and design, entrepreneurship, food, government and law, history, math and computers, and the performing arts as well as those who want to work with their hands or with living things.

Career Ideas for Kids (written by Diane Lindsey Reeves, published by Ferguson)

This series of interactive career exploration books features 10 different titles for kids who like adventure and travel, animals and nature, art, computers, math and money, music and dance, science, sports, talking, and writing.

Careers Without College (published by Peterson's)

These books offer a look at options available to those who prefer to find jobs that do not require a college degree and include titles focusing on cars, computers, fashion, fitness, health care, and music.

Cool Careers (published by Rosen Publishing)

Each title in this series focuses on a cutting-edge occupation such as computer animator, hardware engineer, multimedia and new media developer, video game designer, Web entrepreneur, and webmaster.

Discovering Careers for Your Future (published by Ferguson)

This series includes a wide range of titles that include those that focus on adventure, art, construction, fashion, film, history, nature, publishing, and radio and television.

Risky Business (written by Keith Elliot Greenberg, published by Blackbirch Press)

These books feature stories about people with adventurous types of jobs and include titles about a bomb squad officer, disease detective, marine biologist, photojournalist, rodeo clown, smoke jumper, storm chaser, stunt woman, test pilot, and wildlife special agent.

HEAVY-DUTY RESOURCES

Career encyclopedias provide general information about a lot of professions and can be a great place to start a career search. Those listed here are easy to use and provide useful information about nearly a zillion different jobs. Look for them in the reference section of your local library.

Career Discovery Encyclopedia, 6th ed. New York: Ferguson, 2006.

Careers for the 21st Century. Farmington Hills, Mich.: Lucent Books, 2002.

Children's Dictionary of Occupations. Princeton, N.J.: Cambridge Educational, 2004.

Encyclopedia of Career and Vocational Guidance. New York: Ferguson, 2005.

Farr, Michael, and Laurence Shatkin. *Enhanced Occupational Outlook Handbook.* 6th ed. Indianapolis, Ind.: JIST Works, 2006.

Occupational Outlook Handbook. Washington, D.C.: U.S. Government Printing Office, 2006.

FINDING PLACES TO WORK

Even though you probably aren't quite yet in the market for a real job, you can learn a lot about the kinds of jobs you might find if you were looking by visiting some of the most popular job-hunting sites on the Internet. Two particularly good ones to investigate are America's Job Bank (http://www.ajb.org) and Monster (http://www.monster.com).

INDEX

Page numbers in **boldface** indicate main articles. Page numbers in *italics* indicate photographs.